Married White Male
In Search Of...

Jo Doodle —
Happy Beading.
Treet yourself!
Love—
Mandy

Married White Male In Search Of...

*An Offbeat Look at Family Life,
Faith Life, and Mid-Life*

M A R K   C O L L I N S

LIGUORI/TRIUMPH
LIGUORI, MISSOURI

Published by Liguori/Triumph
An Imprint of Liguori Publications
Liguori, Missouri

Library of Congress Cataloging-in-Publication Data

Collins, Mark.
       Married white male in search of— : an offbeat look at family life, faith life, and mid-life / Mark Collins — 1st ed.
          p. cm.
       ISBN 0-7648-0179-1
       1. Collins, Mark, 1959– . 2. Middle-aged men—United States—Biography. 3. Husbands—United States—Biography. 4. Fathers—United States—Biography. 5. Mid-life crisis—United States. I. Title.
HQ1059.5.U5C655 1998
305.344'081'092—dc21
[B]   97–52263

Excerpts taken from *Daily Guideposts 1998* copyright 1997 by Guideposts, Carmel, NY 10512.

"Dust" copyright 1994 Dorianne Laux. From *What We Carry* (BOA Editions, 1994).

Beth Bateman Newborg's contribution was supported in part by a grant from the Pennsylvania Council on the Arts.

This book about men is dedicated
to the many women in my life:

My mom, my sister, my aunt;

Faith, Hope, and Grace,
my manna from heaven;

And Sandee, who's listed on the bottom
because she holds everything up.
WTK? AY!

Dust

Someone spoke to me last night,
told me the truth. Just a few words,
but I recognized it.
I knew I should make myself get up,
write it down, but it was late,
and I was exhausted from working
all day in the garden, moving rocks.
Now, I remember only the flavor—
not like food, sweet or sharp.
More like a fine powder, like dust.
And I wasn't elated or frightened,
but simply rapt, aware.
That's how it is sometimes—
God comes to your window,
all bright light and black wings,
and you're just too tired to open it.

Dorianne Laux

Contents

Contents

Acknowledgments

The author wishes to thank the following publications where some of these essays first appeared: *The Pittsburgh Post-Gazette*, *Pitt Magazine*, *The Family Therapy Networker*, *The Pitt News*, and *The Pittsburgh Press Sunday Magazine*.

The author wishes to thank Leslie Reimer, Beth Newborg, Carol Mullen, Vicki Glembocki, Anthony Chiffolo, Debra Koma, Jeff Oaks, Alan Friedman, Laura Shefler, Sally Ann Flecker, Ralph, Kris, Mike and Elizabeth, Gary and Megan, Pat Carr, Becky Abromitis, Kevin and Sunny, Brian Doyle, Mary James, Alan Lewis, Susan Kaufmann, Terry and Pauline Tompkins, Rochelle Smith, Helen Short, Bill Isler, Sam Newberry, Fred Rogers, Thomas Buell Jr., Rebecca Redshaw, Jennie Halapatz, and Roberta Kinney for their help. And, with love, to Margaret Mary Corbett and Bro. Joseph Bender, F.S.C.

Foreword

We want to tell stories, we eat stories, stories are how we love and have the courage to go on. Stories are funny and poignant and awful and riveting. Stories are prayers and puzzles. We read them in newspapers, magazines, books like Mark's book cradled in your hand like a small square child, we watch them acted on stage and sound studio, we peer into the stories in paintings and sculptures, we weep and thrill at the stories in music, we are stunned and moved by the stories sudden in the mouths of our startling children—who are themselves stories told by a mysterious and graceful Omniscient Narrator.

We are all storytellers, from our first garbled tales of mud and slugs to our last struggle to shape the words *I love you* in the holy cave of our mouths. "How was school?" our mothers asked, and we told a story, and "Who are you?" our lovers asked, and we told a story, and "What is it you plan to do with your one wild and precious life?" the poet asks, and we tell our stories, day after day after day. We are stories told in the brief light between great darknesses.

In the best stories there is the silver sound of true things said directly, honestly, no fat, cutting to the core of what we are when we are at our best. There is an ancient shape of something true, something that twists up through tragedy and confusion, something true in and of all of us, something that makes us, occasionally, haltingly, holy. Something there is in us divine, and we touch it most and best by story. Once upon a time, we say, this happened to me, and here is the shape of what it means....

Mark Collins tells true stories of cars and love and death and hockey sticks and suicide and diapers and forgiveness and kindergarten and horror and minivans. All are cousins, as love and loss are, and through all his stories there is a thread of delight and courage and mercy that I admire. I hope that you will admire it too.

Brian Doyle

Introduction

My thirties began innocently enough. I was minding my own business, Officer, I *swear*, when Oliver Sudden, several years ago my life hit the gas and never looked back. I was busting loose, leaving tracks, burning rubber, and several other clichés.

I, the nominal driver of this berserk machine, fought desperately for control. Clearly I had hit black ice and was now under the spell of some contrary, terrorizing physics. I smashed both feet into the brake pedal, white-knuckling the steering wheel. Nothing happened. On I went.

I started babbling, hoping that whoever was in control would hear me. (It was difficult to talk; the G-forces pinned my white lips back into my jowls.) "Where did these *kids* come from?" I asked. And "What's all this middle-aged crap? I'm young, I'm young, I'm *young!*"

There was no response. My turbo-charged life sped on, stuck in overdrive, fueled on its own high-octane inertia.

Just as I was making peace with my Maker, I slammed head-on into forty. (Obviously, at that speed, I didn't see it coming.) My head snapped forward, but not brutally—more like the stop on a five-ticket ride at Kennywood rather than a collision you'd see in a driver's ed film. We drifted a few feet forward, then stopped for good.

I checked myself in the mirror. A few more gray hairs, but no blood. Slowly I got out of my life and looked it over. It was hot to the touch and gave off the acrid smell of burned brake pads, but otherwise—miraculously—it was still in one piece.

I pushed it to the side of the road and walked home. It's still sitting there.

I'm thinking now I'd like to try my life again, only this time with a little more control. It may need a jump-start, and I'll probably have to fuss with the throttle. But first I need to take stock; before I can rebuild it, I need to make a careful count of all the greased parts and transmission servos and blown gaskets.

The following essays are the complete inventory. Now that I've finished writing it all down, I realize that this may well be my last book. I cannot imagine another.

So thank you very much for listening.

1

Married White Male...

In a world top-heavy with war, caste, poverty, tyranny, Astroturf, and weirdo cults, it's hard to imagine why anyone would want to write about married white males. Who *cares* if guys seem so troubled? Why do we seem so lost and angry? What is *wrong* with us, anyhow?

Search me. We guys seem genetically incapable of sharing our fears with others. For whatever reason (hubris? upbringing? not enough fiber?), we're cast alone in our little oceans, afloat in our tiny, homemade skiffs, trimming our sails to life's capricious winds, always unable (or unwilling) to seek out better navigation, to pull our boats alee, and—*Gott in Himmel!*—admit we're foundering and call in the Coast Guard or pray to Saint Christopher, patron saint of lost guys....

And yet that same deranged arrogance allows us to weather lousy bosses, erratic cars, rip-roaring hormones, petulant toddlers, and incomplete dreams. For all our insecurity and forced bravado, many men do possess a certain (albeit sometimes misplaced) childish faith. You can see it in their shoulders—the shoulders that their friends can cry on, the shoulders that open recalcitrant garage doors, the shoulders that they put to the work wheel every day. It's the kind of faith found in a man's hardscrabble heart: how he creatively invokes the Lord's name while fixing the plumbing or watching football, yet becomes almost tearfully reverent when watching his daughter's dance recital. It's not a church-going religiosity as much as a tough-guy theology, as valid and complex as any catechism.

The following essays are a look at life at forty, *mit* kids, spouse, and an industrial-strength case of middle-aged angst. It's the '50s skidding off the runway and crashing into the '90s: *Make Room for Daddy on the Therapist's Couch*. The halcyon image of Ward Cleaver at ease with pipe and paper (Lord knows if that image ever *really* existed) has given way to day-care and home repair, to ATMs and MTV. These reflections are the closest I come to soul-searching: looking for God between the lines of life's spontaneous script, finding meaning in my kids' probing, innocent eyes, and making peace with my own Y chromosome.

It's not a Hallmark card, but it's not *Beavis and Butthead* either. God created Man in his own image, Genesis says, and I'm trying to come to grips with this divine paradox: testosterone in tandem with the Almighty.

L'chiam

As I write this, my friends Ralph and Kristi are away celebrating their anniversary. They left their two gorgeous toddlers with the sitter, took off for some time to themselves.

Their wedding was five years ago this month. I remember it well. My wife and I were having a spiteful fight about…well, I can't recall, but something more serious than who left the cap off the toothpaste. Some old hurt hadn't fully healed, and now we stood on opposite ends of our mutual wound, angry, stubborn, digging in for protracted trench warfare. I remember sitting there steaming in the steamy summer heat five years ago when the phone rang. It was Al, the best man for Ralph and Kristi's upcoming wedding. He had planned a bachelor's bash at Three Rivers Stadium, the division-leading Pirates against the hated Cincinnati Reds.

"The bachelor's party is still on," Al began—an interesting opening.

"What do you mean, 'still on'?" I asked.

"You haven't heard?" Al asked.

No, indeed. While my wife and I were busy fighting, Kristi had been rushed to the hospital, a virus slowly paralyzing her from head to toe. A week ago it had been the flu; the night before she was slurring her words. "I'm just tired," she told Ralph. And now, the day before her wedding, she awoke to find her legs didn't work. The complex system of synapses—the same cosmos of nerves and muscles that allowed athletic Kristi to hike river trails, to pedal her mountain bike, to keep up with high school students—had revolted. Al tried to put the best face on the news—she was at Pitt's medical center, in good hands—but his details told a different story. Her arms had gone numb by noon. Already she couldn't talk. If they couldn't stop the spread, she'd need a respirator soon.

"So what's next?" I asked.

"Well, the game begins at seven," Al said.

"No, I mean with *Kristi*. Jeez, Al, the bride's in the hospital but the game goes on, eh?"

Al paused. "Well, it *is* the Reds," he said.

We laughed so hard tears rolled down our cheeks, tears that had been waiting for a manly moment to fall.

The Pirates lost that night, and Ralph never made it to the game. It was more like a wake. We drank our bit-

6

ter beer, laughing spiritlessly, with the untouched nachos growing gamy in the heat. In the seventh inning word came down that Kristi had been diagnosed with Guillain-Barré Syndrome, and doctors at Montefiore were trying plasmapheresis, whereby her blood cells would be "washed" and returned to her. No one knew if it would work.

I knew about Guillain-Barré only because writer Joseph Heller (*Catch-22*) had it. It had nearly killed him; he still isn't walking.

I wondered what would happen to Kris. I wondered why fate dealt such cards, casually tossing a joker on the eve of Kris's wedding. I wondered, too, what had started the fight with my wife. We had drawn our battle lines so quickly, following the familiar rules of marital engagement. But now it seemed so senseless. And as I watched the Pirates lose that night, the final straw snapped. This fine, talented team had suddenly grown awkward and punchless, and I wanted to know why. I wanted to know how everything had soured so quickly.

I wanted to know where reason had gone.

As we bachelor-party-goers filed out of the stadium, sullen, sloppy, our shirts sticking to us in the hanging humidity, nothing much made sense.

The next day we filed into the chapel. Instead of bouquets, the altar was decorated with a large-screen TV. Ralph and Kristi had wed earlier, right there in the hospital room, and we gathered here for the videotape replay. And there it was, homemade footage of Ralph and Al in their tuxedos and Kristi in her hospital gown. The bridesmaid had to read Kristi's vows. And Ralph, who holds the record for physical confrontations by a non-hockey player, choked through his part, stopping twice to weep.

Then the screen went blank. Stunned, some sobbing, we all retreated to the reception hall.

And then something happened. And something also *didn't* happen.

What happened was we partied. We danced. We sang "Devil with a Blue Dress." We told wild stories at Ralph's expense, screaming with laughter. Ralph's mom sang "Sunrise, Sunset." We ate well—a toasted almond torte followed by a champagne toast. And we danced some more, not allowing the band a break. Al ruined his rented tux with champagne and sweat. And somewhere between the aperitif and the speeches, my wife and I laid down our weapons. No more pained looks, sharp glances, steely attitudes. We danced the slow dances. The wound closed. We forgave without words.

But what was magical at this strange wedding was its temperance, what *didn't* happen. Nuptials are meant as celebrations, but every one I've been to has been pockmarked with spats. Aunt Ruthie won't sit next to Uncle Pete, who's mad about the liver pâté. The cake is underdone. The band won't play "Feelings." Stan won't attend because the bride's not Catholic. Cousin Randy is drunk and rowdy.

Not this time. None of that. The videotape kept us sober and attentive. It was as if we all knew the stakes: Celebrate the moment, because next week we might be gathered around a bier, listening to Ralph's mom chant the mourner's kaddish.

But no, no kaddish for Kristi. She's recovered. The only side effect nowadays is a dizzy feeling when she plays too hard with her kids. Her oldest girl likes to play dress-up. When my wife and I bring our kids over to play, Molly disappears into her room and emerges in a wedding dress. And an image flashes before me: I see that wedding again, the one without the bride. I see Ralph atop a chair as we held him aloft. I see it all so clearly now, the cruel and wondrous wedding we celebrated, when we finally understood how precious and fleeting it all is, how unpredictable. One day your team scores ten runs, the next day they're shut out. You never know, but you keep going back. So capricious it's scary. Sad. Amazing. Forgiving. You're so alive.

Happy anniversary, guys. *L'chiam*—to life.

Speak Softly,
and Carry a Hockey Stick

W hen I became a man," Saint Paul writes, "I put
childish things behind me." Some think of Paul
as a visionary. That may be true, but I'll bet he
was a real dullard at parties. The key to adulthood,
I'd argue, is rediscovering all those childish things you
put away and playing with them again, and this time
without those pesky parents watching over you.

Problem is, there aren't enough childish games for
adults. Golf is popular. So is bowling. Neither one ex-
cites me. Golf is the most absurd sport ever invented,
with the possible exception of curling. You hit the ball,
you chase the ball. Hit, chase, hit, chase. When *I* was
growing up, this game was called "having no one else
to play with." I enjoy bowling more, only because I
have the build for it (low to the ground). But the idea

of smashing a bunch of defenseless pins makes me wince. If you get seven out of ten, it's considered a failure. In baseball, you can *miss* seven out of ten and still get paid $1.75 billion.

My sport of choice is dek hockey, which grown men play without skates (and without the *c* in "deck.") It's just like ice hockey, with a regulation-size rink, dasher boards, and referees, except you don't need as much equipment or money or common sense.

Dek hockey games combine a thirty-minute aerobic workout with sticks and swearing—Jane Fonda meets Attila the Hun. I can survive (barely) the aerobic part, and I'm quite facile at swearing. But swinging sticks? No. While "low to the ground" makes me a model bowler, it also puts my noggin in the direct orbit of taller gentlemen in midswing. Many's the time I skillfully stopped a slap shot follow-through using nothing more than my left temple. Even the emergency room doctors called the swelling impressive.

Actually, I'm overselling myself. I am *not* good at the aerobic part. Now in my mid-thirties, I rank as one of the elder participants in a sport clearly designed for a generation too young to remember Gerald Ford. When I first started to play dek hockey again (after a few decades on the disabled list), I'd act as if I weren't really dying from overexertion. After all, that's why (I thought) I played every week—to get in shape, to regain my youth and physique. ("I have the body of a twenty-year-old," Groucho Marx is rumored to have

12

said, "but I have to give it back because I'm getting it all wrinkled.") Now all pretense of fitness is gone. I crawl back to the bench and collapse when my shift is over, screaming for oxygen and a cardiac defibrillator. The other players ignore me as they step over my gasping remains. From this vantage point, I can see vultures circling overhead.

Most galling of all, many of my teammates smoke cigarettes and drink beer after the game. You can do that when you're twenty: your body is endlessly obedient. These guys think nothing of a two-hour practice at midnight, then they'll slam down a few beers, catch a nap before work, and get up and do it again. Me? I sip warm milk as I do the crossword and pad up to bed no later than 11:00 P.M. A little Geritol, some Tommy Dorsey on the Victrola, Mom in her kerchief and I in my cap, and we're asleep by 11:23.

That's what makes hockey so frustrating—and so enticing. I wasn't always this old. I peaked in 1975, but I can still remember it like yesterday, playing three-hour games in the blazing sun or subzero cold, taking breaks only when someone lost an eye or injured a reproductive organ. The score would be something like 17–14, and we wouldn't stop until Joey Marsip's mom called him for dinner, and then we had to quit because he owned the nets. I remember how my body responded then—my vision was better, my reactions quicker, my breathing easier. I could take a pass in full stride, plot my fake around the defenseman, even pick a corner of the net to shoot at. Of course, things rarely went as planned, but the fact that my brain and body had *any* sense of synergy is amazing to me now. Instead, my body and mind have conspired to betray me. Nowadays I carefully set the alarm for 6:00 A.M., full of good intentions to jog a few miles before a healthy breakfast, but then the alarm sounds and my body (well, my hand) slams the clock off and says, "Nobody tells *me* when to wake up!" Another day, another chance at youthful fitness lost.

Or is it?

When I drag my iron-poor blood and bones onto the de(c)k twice a week, is it youthful fitness I'm after? No, not really. I just want a chance to play. As betrayed as I feel, there are those rare magic moments when everything goes magically right. My arthritic joints and myopic eyes occasionally combine to remind me of what I once had, and the young defenseman, startled by my refound prowess, is caught off-guard and out of position. Suddenly, I'm breaking in on the goalie alone, me and my retro-body, and it's like hearing a favorite song after twenty years and I still know all the words. At full stride I dribble the puck, waiting for the goalie to lean one way or the other. I pick a spot to shoot: just below the crossbar, right above his glove. I drag my stick for a second, gathering momentum for the shot, then snap the puck away in a single motion.

And after that, nothing matters. If he makes the

save, then good for him. It's not the goal that counts (though that would be nice), but just the chance to shoot—to reclaim, if only for a second, the sense of my body acting as it once had, and still can: a holy and united sum of its age.

The First Day
of the Rest of Your Life

The first time my father was scared witless was when my sister was born. She was my parents' first child, and unbeknownst to everyone, she decided to navigate the birth canal feet first, her tiny umbilical cord wrapped around her even tinier neck. My father—stationed away from the labor suite like all '50s dads—overheard only two phrases: "emergency cesarean section" and "last rites." His knees, as they say, buckled. (My mother simply asked outright, "Am I going to die?" "No," the doctor said, so my mother returned to her nice dream about Bermuda.)

Everything turned out all right. My sister was born cesarean section, as were my brother and me. We've suffered no permanent damage from the anesthetic, except that we're all excellent nappers.

I was nine when I was first scared witless. My father lay across the bed, clad only in his boxers, his face ashen. He moaned as if gored, alternately clutching the bedpost until his knuckles turned white, then grabbing his head, pulling at his short, military-style haircut. The phrase *writhing in agony* is *not*, I learned, a cliché.

I, of course, thought my father was dying. But, of course, he wasn't. He was passing a kidney stone. Dying would have been much less painful.

In a funny twist of genetic fate, my first-born child would also be a breech-daughter. Thanks to the magic of sonograms, we knew months in advance and prepared for a c-section delivery. And unlike my father, I was allowed to be with my wife in the operating room.

What I *wasn't* prepared for was the sometimes odd reaction to our birth story. "Oh, a *c-section*," some acquaintances (mostly female) would say. "Well, maybe next time…"—meaning maybe next time we'd have a child the *right* way. Others said, "You know, the next one doesn't *have* to be c-section," and it's true: the next one could've been born VBAC (medicalese for "vaginal birth after cesarean"). But she wasn't, thank you. She was born the same cut-and-sew way as her sister. One anesthesiologist said to my wife, "You're one of those unfortunate people who've had a successful c-section and now don't want to try anything else." "Should I apologize?" my wife asked, but her sarcasm was lost on its target.

So here's my simple testosterone-filtered question: why is a c-section not quite the same as a vaginal birth? Is there something transcendent or mythical about the pain of childbirth? Or is it yet another thing that guys just don't get? (Or women who have c-sections don't get, or parents who adopt don't get...)

I keep thinking of my father lying crosswise on the bed. He didn't find his pain to be mythic or transcendent, just unbearable. If someone would've asked, "Would you like for me to anesthetize you, then cut you open and take the stone out?" my father would've gladly agreed.

"Oh, come *on*," you're thinking. "Passing a kidney stone is hardly the same as birthing a baby."

Of course not. One gives you a useless hunk of calcified rock, another gives you a shiny new child. But I'm not talking about the end result, I'm talking about the pain. Guys don't sit around comparing kidney-stone stories. But believe it or don't, they *will* discuss, with hushed awe and respect, the suffering their wives survived in childbirth. (Of course, guys also talk about how much *they* suffered, but that's another story.)

Take away the end result, and what do you have? Pain. Why not talk about the time Aunt Ruthie had her tooth drilled without anesthetic because the dentist just plain forgot? Or why not talk about your sister's successful lumpectomy, and the months of rehab it took to get full motion back in her arm? The tumor was benign—another happy ending—but it's *still* not a story one shares with others: "God, was my sister in pain. Every time she lifted her arm…" Nope, no more party invitations for you. Yet the same party-goers would gladly tolerate a twenty-hours-of-labor-pain story, even a twenty-hours-of-*false*-labor-pain story.

There are several explanations for why childbirth pain seems mythic. I don't like the first two. One is that some women feel the need to justify themselves through pain, that somehow their own existence on this earth isn't enough. Sadly, it's the reason some people have kids in the first place, to "make up" for their own perceived failures. And childbirth pain adds a crowning element of self-sacrifice: *Look what I did for my kids.*

Another explanation is that some people still cling to a twisted form of medieval Catholicism that says pain is good. It's the moral equivalent of pouring sulfa on an open wound: if it hurts, it must be working. Examples abound, mostly stories of people whose lives were forged in the cauldron of suffering, like people who've survived painful divorces and come out stronger. But that's *after* the fact; no one ever says, "I think I'll marry this completely incompatible mate so that I can suffer unspeakable anguish and later (much later) feel better about myself." It's a lesson they wish they had *known,* not one they wanted to have to learn.

The third and best explanation comes by way of my friend Jeff Oaks. Perhaps we're so protected from pain that we're surprised by it and therefore magnify it. Historical ages and other cultures who knew pain knew its role in life. Our age and our culture are comfortable enough that pain and illness are relegated to outsiders, to "the other." If you want to lose friends fast, get a serious illness. Some will rally around you; most will avoid you like...well, like the plague. So something like childbirth pain, which is short-lived and socially redeemed by the child itself, becomes our myth, our legitimized pain, our secular rite of passage.

I think Jeff is right, but there's something else as well. If our culture is more comfortable physically than past generations—and thank God for that—we're not much better emotionally. The shrinks' couches are heaving under the weight of psychic pain. (Shrinks are interesting people. You go to see them because you want a reality check, and the first thing they say is, "Our sessions will be fifty-minute hours." Already they're manipulating time and space. So when they tell you that fifty minutes equals an hour, you tell them that $50 equals $60, and that's all you're going to pay.) Anyway, the shrinks' couches are heaving under the weight of psychic pain. And unlike childbirth, there is no moment, no instant, no hour nor day of pain; our mental anguishes are not singular events. Instead, they're less definable and more ineffable. A shot of Pitocin won't help to induce our recovery. Even Prozac cannot exorcise our demons by itself. It's a daily struggle, a yearly struggle, the battle of a lifetime.

Unlike the piercing but relatively quick pain of childbirth, life's subtle problems are more like slow-growing bamboo shoots beneath the fingernails.

Pain, it turns out, has no purpose in and of itself. My father learned nothing from kidney stones, save that he didn't want one again. Instead, it's what we choose to do in the aftermath that makes all the difference. Intense pain renders us intensely incompetent; when the pain subsides, then we can choose how to act. Pain alone won't make you a better person; pain is mindless—it has no goal. Only you can *choose* what happens next.

In fact, what's forgotten in all this talk about childbirth is what happens next: raising that child. There are tons more classes in Lamaze training, in the husband-coached Bradley Method, and in breathing than there are in parenting. There's no preparation for the pain of a thousand daily decisions and confrontations and lack of sleep and self-doubt and second-guessing that takes place over the next eighteen, twenty-one, forty years. Yes, these moments are tempered by the spontaneous joy that children generate, and the reward of unexpected growth for both grownups and kids alike. But mostly childhood is a series of small, unremarkable moments strung together to make up one young life. Compared to the excitement, the brutal physicality, the sheer exhaustive wallop of childbirth itself, raising kids is pretty boring…and only about ten billion times more important.

Actually, there's another explanation. When I told my friend (a mother of two) this theory, I ended by saying, "I don't know, Kristi, but suffering through childbirth pain when you don't have to seems crazy to me." Kristi smiled diplomatically, and I understood what she wanted to say: *You're right—you don't know.*

And that may be the unkindest cut of all: once again, I'm face-to-face with the chasm of mystery that separates me from the smarter sex. Rationally, I cannot explain why women choose to go through what they do; then again, I can't explain the sometimes-ambiguous joy of parenting, the dumbstruck sense of awe as your kids conquer each amazing milestone, or the ineffable, pervasive feeling of loss in watching your children grow.

I've become familiar with this sense of unfamiliarity. One day, perhaps, I'll understand that certain things will not be understood. Life is a game played the way my kids play, with ever-changing rules and plots, with no fixed focus or reason, played just for the sheer joy (and heartache) of the game itself.

And I've learned to find comfort in the story of Joseph, the foster father of Jesus. I think of him at the moment Mary broke the news: *I am pregnant, and you are not the father. Shall we be married?* I can imagine him leaning against the rickety walls of the stable, exhausted from travel, trying to process the confused wonder of it all. No breathing classes here; no Lamaze. There's no record of what happened when the birth was over, when the shepherds left, so I'll tell you what happened. The new parents made their choice: they wrapped their babe in swaddling clothes and raised it as best they could, on faith and on instinct. And that—like the generations before them and certainly the generations after—turned out to be good enough, another small miracle in an everyday life.

"I'm very much interested in choices and what it is and who it is that enables us human beings to make these choices all through our lives," Fred Rogers of *Mister Rogers' Neighborhood* wrote recently. "What choices lead to ethnic cleansing? What choices lead to healing? What choices led to the chipping away of the Berlin Wall? What helped those Chinese students choose to lie down in front of those tanks in Tiananmen Square?"

What choices do we make every day—choices made out of joy, out of pain, out of suffering? What is it that *we* plan to do with this, the first day of the rest of our lives?

The Long and 42-Short of It

H ere's my impression of the William Henry Harrison administration: *cough, hack, cough, cough, wheeze.* OK, it's a short impression, but it was a short administration. Harrison was president from 1841 to 1841, specifically March to April. (Talk about term limits!) He began his presidency by giving a speech in a rainstorm... and spent the rest of his administration in searching for a cure for pneumonia. (There were no antibiotics then; if Harrison had been alive today...well, he'd be really old.)

I found this factoid while limping along the berm of the Internet superhighway: Siena College Research Institute rated Harrison as the twenty-eighth greatest president, wedged between James A. Garfield, who also died in office, and Herbert Hoover, whom many wished had died in office. (For the record, FDR came in first; Andrew Johnson and Warren G. Harding were last but beat the point spread.) My question is simple: how do you rate a president who was only in office a month? How much damage/good could he do in thirty days, many spent abed?

I don't know the researchers at Siena, but I'll bet a pocketful of dead presidents that they're male. Guys love numbers (except when it comes to anniversaries and checkbook balances; no one can explain this). Ask a guy to remember who's Secretary of the Treasury or even one Romantic poet, and he'll draw a blank; ask him the size of his car's engine or the top three teams on any football poll, and he'll remember it all verbatim. It's a gift or a burden, depending on whom you talk to.

So you can imagine my confusion a few years ago when my wife received a clothing catalog with a big note that said, "ANNOUNCING OUR NEW SIZES— SEE INSIDE." And, sure enough, there was a chart that resized every piece of clothing: size 10 was now size 8; 22 had become 18.

I immediately understood the strategy: make women feel better by making them feel smaller. ("Do you like this new jacket? It's a size 6, and it fits like a glove!")

Guys don't go for that. You don't see men's catalogs that say, "ANNOUNCING OUR NEW TROU-

SER SIZES! IF YOU WERE 34 WAIST/34 INSEAM, YOU'RE NOW 30/30." Any self-respecting man would get his .30-.30 and shoot that catalog to smithereens. (Most men can't figure out the metric system, so how do you think they'd cotton to someone retooling their waist size?) Women who are big and tall shop at stores called "Pretty Plus" or "Fashions for the Fuller Figure." Big and tall men shop at stores called "The Big and Tall Men's Store." If a guy found a jacket marked 40-regular and he's a 44-short, I got news for you: *he wouldn't even try it on*. Why? Cause it's not his size. So you'll never find a man who says, "Son of a B! I can fit into a 40-regular!" It just won't happen.

What started me on all of this? Another women's clothing catalog, this one from Victoria's Secret. Sandee has ordered from them occasionally, and that's all you need to do to get a new catalog every other day. So she was perusing the lingerie, and I was, ahh, helping her. (You know, like helping her to turn the pages and stuff. Honest.) Anyway, I remarked that becoming a lingerie model must be the pinnacle of a model's career. Nope, my wife said. These models would never grace the pages of *Vogue* or *Glamour* or prance down the runways in Paris. Lingerie models are way too meaty for such work. Parisian fashion models are much thinner.

Now this surprised me.

The women in the catalog appeared to be in fine shape. I couldn't *imagine* saying to any one of 'em, "Gosh, sweetheart, you're *way* too meaty for me. Lose some weight!" But I've since had the chance to see *Vogue* and *Glamour,* and my wife is right. We're talking thin. Good-looking, mind you, but skinny with a capital *I.*

Human being-type people come in all shapes and colors and formats. Standards of beauty are arbitrary and ever-changing, from Rubenesque to the early Elvis. Some cultures bejewel their naked bodies; others cover themselves from head to toe. Our society's differing definitions of "model" is just one more bit of evidence that beauty really is in the eye of the beholder.

Whoa, there, Ranger Rick, you're thinking, *if beauty really* is *in the eye of the beholder, then that forty bucks I blew on skin exfoliant is really wasted. I mean, the next person I'm attracted to might* enjoy *unfoliated skin...*

Bingo. There's no accounting for some people's tastes (and thank God for that or I wouldn't be married). Each day is a battle between us and our smarter selves. We know that our moms were clichéd but correct—beauty really is more than skin deep, yet there we are, plunking down our VISA cards for a pair of platform shoes.

A friend of mine recently confided to me her life-long battle with anorexia. If you saw my friend, this news would stun you, because she is stunning. She knows, in her head, that her anxiety about weight is misplaced, yet she cannot wrestle that thought, that *fact,* into her heart. And every day another catalog or magazine arrives in her mailbox, full of retouched photographs and other impossibilities. So everyday the conflict flares between her head and her heart; what should be an enjoyable piece of French toast becomes instead a decision, a question, an internal combat full of sound and fury, signifying nothing.

Maybe the secret is to first forgive ourselves our less-than-optimal weight, our out-of-proportion height, our imperfect skin, our lousy eyesight. No, it doesn't excuse us from eating right or exercising, but it may relieve us of the ridiculous fashion fads that make us feel…well, less than heaven-sent. Because, by God, that's *exactly* what we are.

Kids 'n Cars, Part One

Ever since 1991—May 9, in fact, when my first daughter was born—my life has rolled along as smoothly as a broken-down Rambler. All my free time (*free time!* HAHAHAHAHAHAHAHA) is spent on two recurring themes, themes that should never be paired together:

Kids and cars.

Like oil and water, like an old married couple that should've divorced years ago but somehow forgot, kids and cars do not mix.

Here's one example: despite claims to the contrary from manufacturers, there has yet to be a car built that's kid-friendly. There are, of course, some built-in disadvantages. First, seats. All cars have a place to sit (sometimes several), and kids don't like to sit, so *ipso fatso,* we've got a problem. Unbeknownst to adults, manufacturers stud the seat cushions with steel burrs that can be felt only by a kid's bottom, so kids will practically do anything but sit in their car seats. Instead, they'll execute escapist acts rivaling those in *The Shawshank Redemption,* performing contortions that could stump Houdini. And even better than Houdini, kids perform their magic with a stomach full of whine.

So you'd think the answer would be to get something less confining—like a van. And car dealers would like nothing better—which is why their van ads always feature smiling families the likes of whom you've never met. (I hardly ever smile when I say to my three-year-old daughter, "GET IN THE CAR AND GIVE BACK YOUR SISTER'S TONSILS RIGHT NOW!") But vans simply give kids a larger venue for roaming. The premise of the movie *Home Alone* may seem ludicrous—how could anyone lose a child?—but it's easy in a van. One moment Junior is squirming out of his car seat, the next moment he's underneath the spare tire. Or hidden between pages 34 and 35 of the owner's manual, and you've never even *looked* there. Or playing craps in Vegas with the $367.15 worth of *your* change he found between the seat cushions. Sure beats playing Padiddle.

So others choose the friendly confines of a station wagon. Wrong again. The trunk (or "wayback," as it's often called) is rarely used for its intended purpose of hauling groceries or tailgating. Instead, it serves as a staging area for countless acts of mayhem, occasional arson, and noise levels well above those heard at Bikini Atoll. Like all fathers, I've learned the skill of driving with my left hand while looking into the rearview mirror to seek out the guilty party and mete out a right-handed punishment. ("IF YOUR SISTER CAN'T HAVE HER TONSILS, THEN NO ONE CAN HAVE TONSILS!") Kids who escape to the wayback can pretty much commit felonies without any fear of retribution until, of course, they arrive at Grandma's, where they receive chocolate-chip cookies as punishment.

I digress, but you see the problem: While I can handle squeaky brakes, I can't handle squeaky kids. I can direct my daughters to their bedroom, but I can't direct electricity into a busted alternator. I can sometimes be a good parent, sometimes a good mechanic, but not both simultaneously. SO WHY DOES THE VAN BREAK DOWN THREE MILES FROM THE DANCE RECITAL, AND THREE MILES FROM MY TOOLS? What is God trying to tell me? Once, I was so angry at my car I swung at it with the handle end of a Phillips screwdriver. I missed the car and struck myself on the noggin.

It's a conspiracy.

After years of searching, I have found a solution: buy a U-Haul van. (U-Haul is a registered trademark of somebody somewhere, so don't take it for yourself.) Depending on size, you can either keep your kids safely isolated in a small but attached room, or get a separate trailer that's so big your offspring may as well be in another zip code. And no worries about messy cleanup—just turn on the garden hose full force and everything is spotless.

In fact, you could probably clean up the van that way, too.

Eulogy for Eppa Rixey

I came to praise Eppa Rixey, not to bury him. They already buried him when he died in 1963.

Now I know you're asking, "Just who the H-E-double-hockey-sticks is Eppa Rixey?"

He was a baseball pitcher. For twenty-one years he toiled in Philadelphia and Cincinnati, pitching nearly 4,500 innings. In 1922 he won twenty-five games, the best in the National League. Of course, in 1917 he *lost* twenty-one games, the worst record in the league. All in all, Eppa Rixey won 266 games, which is mighty respectable. Then again, he also lost 251 games. Only four gentleman have ever lost more games than Eppa Rixey.

And here's the kicker: he's in the Hall of Fame, right between Phil Rizzuto and Sam Rice.

Now that you know who he is, you're asking another question: "How the H-E-double-hockey-sticks did Eppa Rixey get into the Hall of Fame?"

Well, why not? I say good for Eppa Rixey. OK, so maybe his only claim to fame is that he hung around for so long. That's no mean feat. Win or lose, on good days and bad, Eppa Rixey went out and pitched his innings. He didn't strike out that many, but he didn't walk many either. He was just another working guy from Culpepper, Virginia, trying to make a living at something he loved.

And now he's mostly forgotten. And that's too bad, because we should honor people like Eppa Rixey. May 3, his birthday, should be a national holiday for all those working folks who do nothing more admirable (and nothing less admirable) than shoulder their adequate talent and make a living. It's not a celebration of the mediocre (mediocre folks don't play for twenty-one years) but of those who do a fine if unremarkable job. We have statues and buildings and entire streets named after some really average presidents, why not a day for the rest of us, whose only amazing feat is that we survived?

So, next May 3, shout, "Happy Eppa Rixey Day!" Celebrate by doing nothing more extraordinary than being yourself. Now *that* is extraordinary.

Hitting the F-Note

When I was growing up, my dad used to spare us kids the curses he had honed in the Navy. When he slammed his thumb with a hammer, he'd scream, "GOD..." and there would be a pause as he altered the course of his oath at the last possible moment: "GOD...*BLESS* OUR HAPPY HOME!" he'd wail.

We had a wooden plaque in our basement that said exactly that: a head shot (well, painting) of Jesus on a particularly stern day. "God Bless Our Happy Home," it read, though you suspected it was more of a request than a statement of current conditions.

My mother, on the other hand, didn't utter a curse until I was...I dunno, in college, I guess, by which time she had plenty to swear about. The strongest condemnation she could use was "I'm *provoked* at you!" which hit us like a slap in the face. My brother and sister and

I would quake. It meant she was *really* incensed, and we were grounded for the millennium.

So it was with this familial background that I chuckled at the public outcry over Greg Lloyd and his F-note a few years ago. Lloyd, a linebacker for the Pittsburgh Steelers, had just come from an excruciating 20–17 win over the Indianapolis Colts and was caught on TV saying, "We're going to the freakin' Super Bowl!"

Only he didn't say "freakin'."

Within minutes, local talk-show phones lit up, and letters appeared in the newspaper. "A poor role model" came in first; "black eye on the city" was second but beat the point spread. Lloyd seemed bewildered by the attention but did not appear especially apologetic.

I say good for Greg Lloyd.

Now I'm not suggesting that we all start freakin' swearing in public, just to show some unity against the Puritans. It's sort of like barfing: it's simply not a nice thing to do in polite company, tossing your blue language all over Aunt Agatha's new white rug.

In fact, that's the whole *point* of a healthy obscenity—finding the right time and place. Use it too much or too inappropriately, and the curse loses its bite. "This sucks" has wormed its way into the lexicon and raises nary an eyebrow anymore. Taking the Lord's name in vain hardly rates a PG-13. So we're left with just a few words that still retain some venom, and Greg Lloyd used one of them.

Perhaps I'm sympathetic because swearing—like spitting and scratching—is such a prototypical guy thing. (I've noticed more women swearing, and it just doesn't fit them as well. Sort of like neckties. Don't ask me why.) I guarantee that cursing was developed by a guy, probably way back in the Pleistocene era. ("Man, it's cold. I wish we were evolved enough to make a damn fire.") And it's been passed on through the Y chromosome ever since.

Shakespeare, for instance, is full of immoderate oaths. No plain "SOB" for the Bard. *Lear*'s Kent calls Oswald "the son and heir of a mungril bitch." General Sherman didn't burn down Georgia saying, "War is heck." *Gone With the Wind* would've been mighty lame to end on, "Frankly, my dear, I don't give a fig." Army officer A. C. McAuliffe may have replied, "Nuts" when the Nazis demanded his surrender at Bastogne, but my guess is that his reply came in two words. And, some Bible scholars argue, Jesus' admonishment to Peter, "Get thee behind me, Satan!" may actually be a kind translation of an Aramaic phrase meaning "Go to hell." (And Jesus could send you there, too.)

Admittedly, American males swear under less extreme situations than war or leaving Vivian Leigh. We cuss wherever we can, no matter what the occasion. ("Why is his sermon so freakin' long?") But instead of chalking it up to another example of how guys are so ig-nernt, think of it as a release valve for all that goes wrong in a typical guy's life. To be a guy is to be eternally exasperated by cars, kids, work, spouse, traffic, referees, lottery picks, broken furnaces, broken dreams, spilled coffee, the slings and arrows of outrageous fortune, and the IRS. That pretty much takes up every waking hour, except for eating and bathroom breaks. (You'll notice men don't swear when they're chewing or sh...um, showering.) Give a man a tune-up for his Chevy and he'll swear at the bill; teach a man to tune-up his Chevy and he'll swear at his purple thumb. I dunno—it's instinct. It's innate. It's freakin' genetic.

And maybe that's why Greg Lloyd's utterance seemed so apropos. He earned it. We don't want our kids to swear because it sounds so foolish and unbecoming in a child. Adolescents cuss because dirty words are like new toys, and besides, it angers the adults. Lloyd, on the other hand, said what he *should* have said, what a lot of guys were thinking. It was the camera operator's fault, not Lloyd's. He was frozen there on an emotional apex, his entire professional life culminating in this rarest of moments. It was every fan's dream, and he was living it. He reached back for words of wonder and found the closest ones available. Sure, they were about as literate as "nuts," but they had the same unadorned bang. He *deserved* his phrase, his moment; the camera happened to catch him in the act. Blame the lack of a ten-second delay, blame the television director, but don't blame Lloyd.

Which reminds me of my dad. On one momentous occasion when I was about thirteen, I was helping him fix a leaking pipe in the basement (right near the plaque of You-Know-Who). With one loud grunt, my father overtightened a valve nut and cracked the casing. Above the din of cascading water I heard my old man say, "GOD...," then his pause, then, "DARN!"—only he didn't say darn. While we went in a frantic search for rags to tie around the split pipe, I was thinking, *That's it. I have arrived. I have not been spared, I have not been condescended to. I have joined the choir of off-color arias, the men's club, the club of the curse.*

Well, I'll be darned.

Reinventing Myself

My wife, Sandee, and I recently rented the movie *The Scarlet Letter* on video. Everything happens exactly as it does in Nathaniel Hawthorne's book, only differently. For instance, Demi Moore's Hester Pryne spends a lot of time frolicking in the buff (instead of in New England). And instead of the red letter "A" standing for adultery, it stands for advance publicity. Oh, and it has a happy ending. (The original, you may recall, was about as cheery as a *really* rough prostate exam.)

Changing the facts of classic tales is an intriguing idea. Imagine:

Instead of *Hamlet*'s dead-bodies-everywhere plot line, Hamlet's father could be a *friendly* ghost, like Casper. "The feel-good movie of the year," says Rex Reed.

Instead of blinding himself, Oedipus could just take

out one of his eyes, leaving him with a really neat eye patch, like John Wayne's in *True Grit*.

The Joads' journey to California should be remade into a car chase, preferably with Sharon Stone as Ma Joad and Jim Carrey as Tom. And at the end, there could be a terrific wreck with flames and explosions and slo-mo.

Who wants to watch another rerun of Ken Burns's *The Civil War* during a pledge break? If PBS wants to rake in some money, threaten to alter the ending: "Well, folks, it's Day Three at Gettysburg, and Pickett is lining up his troops. Call 1-900-US-GRANT if you want the Union to repel the attack; call 1-900-IM4-DIXIE to teach those Yankees a lesson. $3.95 a call, and all tax-deductible."

I'm the king of revising history—at least my family will tell you that. According to them, the personal history I write is loaded with errors, outright fantasy, or simple omission. While I sometimes condense a scene here or there, or alter a quote or two (usually some paint-by-numbers touch-up on the blue language), I swear what I write is true. Every word.

Thus you see the problem: one family, one event, but two or three different memories. With little in the way of objective evidence, we're left to sort out who's right among our conflicting recollections.

When I first recognized this pattern of divergent memories, I, of course, assumed my accounts were the correct ones. After all, as the youngest of the family, my neurons were strong and vital and less warped from age. This hubris worked until I was confronted with people younger than myself—friends or students who would remind me of something I had said in class, something I had absolutely no memory of ever uttering. (My friend Alan recently told me, "It's so true what you said about writers—no one ever asks a lawyer, 'Did you do some lawyering today?' But a writer is supposed to write *every day*. Why? If you write once a day or once a decade, you're still a writer." And I thought, *Did I say that? Well, good for me!*) Therapists talk about "mythmaking" in families—how stories in families take on mythic proportions. Everyone knows some version of this: Great Granddad once shook hands with Abraham Lincoln's cousin, but by the time the story filters through the generations he took one of Booth's bullets at Ford's Theater.

Take, for instance, the line above, the one about PBS and Gettysburg. My brother first used that line, but he claims *I* came up with it. Then there was the time I turned to Sandee and said, "You talkin' to *me?*"

And she said, "What's that from?"

And I said, "*Taxi Driver.*"

And she said, "I never saw it."

And I said, "We saw it together."

And she said, "That must've been your other wife."

No. It was her. I remember talking about it in the parking lot. We were in the 'vette. OK, maybe it was a

Chevette, not a Corvette, but still...oh, what's the use of trying to convince her that she saw it?

Maybe there's a reason we recreate the past. My family is so swamped with shared history—the time the car broke down on a family vacation, and my father, beside himself with misery, began to whistle hysterically; another vacation, when a beachcomber mentioned casually to my parents that a two-year-old (me) was submerged in a tidal pool and hadn't moved in a while—that our retold stories have become legion and legend. Who can tell, with the remove of so many years, what's real or not? What matters is the essence: the car that drove my father to madness, the vacation when Mark almost drowned. The rest is mere detail, colors to fill in the cartoon background.

And so these stories grow arms and legs and strut their way around our dinner conversations. As they age, they become clumsy and unwieldy, but we don't care as long as they fit in the room; as long as they entertain us, they can be any size or shape or color. The goal isn't accuracy but to categorize family lore so that the story—the Big Story, the Story of Who We Are—can be told again and again. There's nothing inherently funny about my nearly drowning in Ocean City, but the story imparts grace and redemption to those anxious moments when my father reached into the water and pulled me up, and I sputtered and coughed, back on dry land, back among the living, back within my family, full of stories to tell.

The Eyes Have It

I once missed a job opportunity because of poor eye contact. The interviewer called to give me the bad news, and she mentioned—unsolicited—that I had failed to look at her square.

"I understand," I told her, but I really didn't. It struck me then as *her* problem; I'm a writer, for God's sake, so how much eye contact is necessary?

Now I'm not so sure. My kids—three little girls, each with enormous, blue-startled eyes—have taught me something about staring, about seeing past the corneas and irises. Their pupils search my inner recesses, seeking answers or wisdom or something else I'm short on. It's disconcerting when a simple request for Juicy Juice becomes a soulful moment.

And, I've found, it's not just me. In an unscientific survey, I've discovered that adult males have lousy eye contact. Oh, sure, when the conversation hinges on work or cars or the Knicks, they'll look at you dead-on. But raise the emotional level—birth, death, love, mothers-in-law—and they look away. Suddenly, they'll search the floors for answers, or stare at the cabinets, the ceiling, ESPN—anything but the questioner's eyes.

Girlfriends and wives have good eye contact, and nine times out of ten they're female, to boot. ESPN tends to play a lesser role in their lives, thus increasing their odds of bringing up a stare-down subject like family or commitment.

So kids and girlfriends and wives are better...I dunno, *lookers*. OK, guys can live with that. Maybe guys have dysfunctional eye muscles from their traditional roles as hunter-gatherers. Guys might have trouble looking at you when discussing public versus private school for little Becky, but he has *no* trouble looking straight into a muskie's isinglass eyes as he reels it aboard. (Hot damn!)

But no, that's not it, either. Women who are not girlfriends or wives or kids can still reduce men to anxious avoidance. I'm speaking here of strippers—not that I'd actually *know*, but from what I've been told. With one glance, strippers—the good ones, at least—have an innate ability to find that slice of your soul you'd forgotten or never knew you had. They smile at you as they grind away, and lock their eyes on your past—that first time your prepubescent self discovered the magic of The Other. Even at that tender age—eleven? twelve?—you knew, immediately and forever, that you wanted to feel it again. You've discovered, over time, to be suspicious of those with soul-stealing stares. Love, is turns out, is like a finely tuned wine, wet and sensual, something to be sipped and savored over time. Lust is alcoholism—binge drinking, totally out of control. And staring—the kind done by strippers and others encountered by chance—is crack cocaine: the moment it hits you, nothing else matters. You love it as much as you hate it, hate its power. And you want more.

Ironic, eh? How men gravitate to the eyes from which they hide? Women, even four-year-old women, have this power of men. It's the intensive stare of intimacy that men seek to escape, but to which they return, again and again, like masochistic moths to the hot flame. Nothing in a man's life—not their jobs, not sports, not even cars—demands such depth. Not even a '74 Plymouth with a bad idle requires *this* much maintenance...

So whatever it is that women want with their heart-rending stares, you can have it. I'm no match for you. Feel free to look deep into my eyes—just move a little to the left so I can still see the game.

Life's a Beach

On vacation, everything is present tense. Problem is, most men—and I speak here in sweeping generalizations because...well, because I can—most men are wary of a day without agenda, let alone a whole *week*. No alarm clocks, no meetings, no grass to cut. If you've ever seen a man walking along the beach, kids in tow, staring vacantly out to sea, you'd think *He seems so happy.* He is anything but. He's content, mind you—a bad day on vacation beats a good day at work by two touchdowns—but men on vacation are men confused. Leisure makes them restless. They'd rather be golfing, where one follows strict rules of engagement. Or watching baseball, where other men follow strict rules etc. Last week, when they were back at the office with too much to do, these same men were fantasizing about the beach, about sleeping in, about sitting on the deck reading the latest John Grisham.

By Day Two they've grown bored with the book, they're tired of sand everywhere (including the private parts of their swim trunks), and they're fantasizing about having something to do. Right about then they might reach for a cold Rolling Rock, even though it's a tad shy of 11:00 A.M. What the heck, it's vacation.

Men can be strong. Men can be decisive. Men can be laconic. Ironic. Neurotic. Iambic. Men can be drunk.

But they cannot simply *be*. It's against their nature.

I'm writing this at 11:00 A.M. on a beautiful summer day in Avalon, New Jersey, a suburb of the Atlantic Ocean. Unlike the uncivil terrain of hometown Pittsburgh, Avalon is a magically horizontal place where one can truly witness the curvature of the Earth. Out there past the sailboats, past the jet skis at $70 an hour, past my two young children swimming beyond the breakers (HEY! GET BACK HERE NOW!), lies the vast ocean, the cradle of life. Out of this ancient water, unchanged since Genesis, the first form of land animal stumbled out of the sea—and he was male, no doubt, because he was obviously *lost*. Undeterred and unwilling to ask for directions, he began to breathe the foreign air, began to crawl across the sand, began a slew of new species. And I'll bet the first thing my Carboniferous cousin said was "Now what?"

Men cannot *be* present tense. They can reminisce (a dangerous practice, usually involving their tryout with the JV soccer team or a rehashing of some bad karma with a long-ago lover); they can be forward-thinking, albeit delusional ("One day, by God, I'll march into his office and *demand* a raise!"), but to be firmly here-and-now, to attend fully to their child's sand-castle, to revel in this outrageous gift of nature, to simply enjoy the ride without noticing that suspicious noise near the right front wheel after spending all that money on a new front end and if they think I'm paying for a new CV boot they have another thing coming just how dumb do they think I am?

Nearby, my four-year-old is chasing a seagull. The seagull flies away, but not before nabbing a clam. The gull rises twenty feet in the air, then drops the shell onto the hard sand to break it apart. Other birds, alerted by the cracked shell, close in to steal a meal. (Despite their reputation as gentle, fun-loving birds, seagulls are scavengers, city pigeons in drag.) A battle ensues over the poor clam, who's jerked around among half a dozen beaks.

Seagulls don't enjoy their food.

I think they're all male.

It's 11:00 A.M. on the last Saturday of vacation, and I'm parked on the Atlantic City Expressway, one cog in a giant traffic jam. The sea of cars looks to be made up of badly cloned copies—oddments of mini-vans and station wagons with bikes on the roof rack, suitcases and beach chairs in the wayback, a cooler full of Juicy Juice and sandwiches growing gamy in the heat. We men are at the wheel, cursing the toll booth at the Walt Whitman Bridge. ("Paying two bucks to *leave* Philadelphia is one thing, but paying two dollars to get in...")

But it's not just the traffic. Toward the end of the week at the beach, an unaccustomed feeling crept over us, what women and other normal people call "relaxation." One day (was it Thursday? What day *is* it?), we woke up and forgot to be preoccupied, forgot to read the box scores, forgot to call in for messages. For a day or so we became just *us,* just guys on the beach, doing nothing and doing it well. Our ordered brains plunged into Zen-like free-fall—no plan, no program, no objective other than to build the perfect castle with a four-year-old here on the sand, here and now, here at the lip of the cradle of life...

...and you're lost in this exquisite thought until the Taurus station wagon behind you beeps, and you're on your way across the bridge, across the Delaware River, across the water that washes into the eternal sea, until you do it all again next year.

2 Good 2 B 4 Gotten

Everyone suspects themselves of at least one cardinal virtue," says Nick Carraway in Fitzgerald's *The Great Gatsby*. This is mine: When it come to keeping secrets, I am supremely trustworthy.

Why this quality? It could be that I am morally superior. Upright. Virtuous. My heart is so pure, I have the righteousness of two men. I am the Righteous Brothers.

Or it could be that my memory is shot. Gone. *Finis*. Blank. "Forgive and forget," the saying goes, but I just skip the first part and go right to the second.

In the course of thirtysome years (I can't remember my exact age), I've forgotten the Alamo, the *Maine,* 1977, new math, the principles of Keynesian economics, the Monroe Doctrine, the Gettysburg Address, my address, and my wife's wedding dress. (I was supposed to pick it up from the cleaners in 1983.) I can't remember the Four Horsemen of the Apocalypse, the Twelve Days of Christmas, or the fifty ways to leave your lover.

What's frightening is what *has* survived on my mental hard drive. While key dates and times have disappeared—anniversaries, birth dates, the days of the week ending in *y*—I've retained the entire 1968 St. Louis Cardinals' lineup. I can remember all the lyrics to "Hey, Hey, We're the Monkees." I remember every nuance of numerology connected to my first car: a 1969 Olds Delta 88 Royale—an eight-cylinder three-speed with a 454-cubic-inch engine. Two-barrel carburetor. Yessir.

Meanwhile I have *no* idea where my present-day car is parked, or whether it's gym day for my five-year-old. She needs to wear tennis shoes on gym day, but some mornings I just slap on the tennies even if she's wearing a dress, just to cover my bases.

My name is Mark, and I am mnemonically deficient.

I have developed an intricate and elaborate system of memory devices. I recently purchased software for my computer that lists my daily tasks and appointments. In the breast pocket of my jacket is my week-at-a-glance calendar. I have Post-It Notes posted everywhere, in virtually every free space in my office. (Post-It Notes are a registered trademark of somebody, but I can't remember whom.)

Yet my memory, though handicapped, can still outwit this complex scheming. My calendar *is,* in fact, in my jacket pocket...and my jacket is safely at home—hanging on the back door so I wouldn't forget it. (Yeah, right.) The yellow Post-It Notes have lost all meaning; they now crowd my desk like a saffron collage, so no single note is notable (or readable). And the software... what a joke. Unbeknownst to me, each daily task that I carefully list on my computer stays there until I finish *all* my duties. I can't tackle tomorrow's list until I finish today's—sort of a digital version of my third-grade teacher. In other words, when I finish this essay, I can cross it off my to-do list...which is now six weeks old.

I've added something new to my to-do list: *Buy different scheduling software.*

Despite these troubles, there is some good news. Three things, actually.

First, a lousy memory makes for great friendship. Instead of a photographic memory, I have the memory of a photographer's assistant: I can airbrush away the mistakes, the parts of the picture that are better left unseen. My brother recently (and bravely) apologized to me for some long-ago slight. I assured him that the matter was forgotten—and I couldn't have been more sincere.

Second, I'm much more appreciative of the wonder around us. While those who can remember today's forecast bring their umbrellas, I'm free of such accoutrements. Okay, I'm a little wet, too, but a quick walk in a stiff rain can be bracing. Besides, I can change into dry tennis shoes back in my office—I forgot to take them home yesterday.

And third...well, I can't remember what it is, but I'll bet it had something to do with spontaneity. I've paid dearly for the things I've lost and have spent much of my adult life searching for little slips of paper containing crucial phone numbers. But I've also spent some wonderful moments with my kids because I forgot to be somewhere else. I once went camping in the middle of the week, blissfully unaware that I was also missing a momentous meeting at work.

But guess what? Life went on. I apologized profusely, yet I regretted nothing. Oh sure, maybe I had forgotten to take a few things to the campsite—a lantern would've been nice, and some tent stakes—but I had a good time nonetheless.

And I forgot all about work, too. I may go back to that campground some time. It was...*north* of here, I think, or maybe east. I had a map around here somewhere...

Redoing the Inside

After our second child was born, my wife hinted that we needed a bigger house. Always a tactful woman, she'd say something subtle like "Even the searing pain of childbirth was better than this lousy kitchen." When I failed to take the bait, she upped the ante by introducing me to her friends as "my first husband, Mark."

With mortgage rates finally dropping below usury levels, we decided to refinance the house and put the extra cash ($17.28) into renovation. After an exhaustive search, we found a suitable contractor—someone crazy enough to accept both our credit and our offer to do as much of the work ourselves as we could.

As we talked about the new kitchen, I began to reinvent myself. In my imagination I wasn't a carpentry novice, but someone who spoke eloquently of joists and mortar and headers. I wore safety glasses and steel-toed shoes, and I drove a pickup truck. My name was no longer Mark but "Skip," and I could easily transform an ordinary broom closet into a split-level condo with a wet bar, using nothing more than a Swiss Army knife and a catcher's mitt.

But reality returned with a thud as Bob the contractor gave me my first job: removing nails from old boards.

Actually, Bob didn't give me the job as much as I involuntarily volunteered. To save money, I suggested we reuse the old beams and 2 x 4s in the new kitchen. Bob agreed, but only as long as I pulled out the old nails. This was, after all, the kind of skill-less, labor-intensive task I had asked for. Besides, Bob said, it kept me away from more dangerous jobs like plumbing.

I thought pulling nails might take the better part of a Sunday afternoon, but it took the better part of my free time for a week. How difficult could it be to pull a few nails, you ask? First, it was more like a few *hundred* nails, and second, nails are designed to make their removal difficult. That's their whole point, if you pardon the pun. And my kids didn't help; they insisted that I jump in the leaves with them *right now*. (When a two-year-old pulls on your pinkie to get you to move, it's useless to argue. I'd say, "Daddy has to work," but it fell on deaf ears. "Jump more time" was her only reply.)

My nail-removal technique was awkward, as I alternately yanked and cursed with a variety of claw hammers and pliers. Every nail fought extradition, and some required special surgery. Then I discovered Bob's mini-crowbar, and things got much easier. I developed a rhythm: hammer the point of the nail, turn the beam over, pull the head up, then use the crowbar's claw to pry the nail out. Hammer, turn, pull, pry, hammer, turn, pull, pry. It became a little song: BANG! ZZZIIIPP! SQUEAK! then PING! as I flung the bent nail into the empty can of Juicy Juice. My confidence resurfaced. OK, maybe I wasn't ready for anything complicated like hanging wallpaper, but at least I knew my way around a crowbar.

That little victory was quickly crushed by my next assignment: sanding the plaster "mud" that joined the sheets of drywall. How hard could it be? I had patched and sanded a dozen cars, so I thought I had the knack.

After a weekend of continuous sanding, my hair and eyebrows white from plaster dust and my shoulders aching, Bob came in on Monday morning. He rubbed his palm against my handiwork, then picked up the sandpaper. Eight hours later, the kitchen choked in a fine white fog, he pronounced the walls were *finally* ready to paint.

Cowered by the sanding fiasco, my wife and I painted as if our egos depended on it, which they did. We taped, we stirred, we critiqued each other's work, and never let an errant drop of paint fall errantly (save for the jelly jar of primer that spilled when Thomas the Train derailed from my daughter's hand and skidded across the floor).

But Bob seemed pleased—meaning he didn't redo it. Our next task, he said, was staining all of the new woodwork.

Buoyed by our painting success, I was eager to start. After thirty minutes, I was just as eager to stop. Staining combines the tedium of sanding with the monotony of pulling nails and the precision of painting. It's careful, boring work. And it's twice as difficult when a one-year-old insists that you stop every few minutes to rewind Big Bird's jack-in-the-box or fix the two-year-old's Big Wheel.

The worst part of staining is the fumes, which cause both hallucinations and cancer, sometimes simultaneously. I began to have LSD-like apparitions, imagining the kitchen was actually finished, imagining washing dishes in a sink instead of a bathtub, imagining a time when I wouldn't have to sprint across the room to remove another piece of building material from my daughter's mouth. ("No, honey, no more galvanized nails. You'll ruin your dinner.")

In time—ever, *ever* so slowly—white pine became dark pine became varnished dark pine. With the can of stain resealed, my head began to clear, and I could see the progress. In fact, it wasn't just "progress" but an epiphany. While I was busy pulling nails, Bob had dismembered an entire wall. While I was sanding, a new floor had appeared. I stained the last of the woodwork by the light of the morning sun pouring through the new windows. While I had been busy cursing, a new kitchen had arisen around me. Unable to lift my eyes from the work, I hadn't seen how far we had come, only what was yet to be done.

In those intervening months, other things had happened. My youngest daughter began to walk. My oldest daughter learned her ABCs and how to count to twenty (though she mysteriously excludes the number fifteen). Sure, I had noted each milestone, but I had failed to connect the dots. Kids aren't just milestones and events but an ever-shifting series of moments, urgent and alive every day.

That's the thing about childhood: it takes forever to go by so quickly. While I was about my manly work, my children, in a wisdom born of innocence, insisted that I do my real job—acting like Daddy, albeit a distracted one. Neither child seemed to mind the mess nor the money. As long as I can repair a trike or retape the torn pages of *Clifford's Bathtime* or sing "Put Down the Duckie" on demand, then I'm an OK home-repairman.

And that's OK with me. I may be an awkward parent—unsanded, unvarnished, unready—but I'm learning. I'll probably never get the joists even or the walls plumb, but for now, everything is either in place or at least on schedule, and I'm learning how to step back and admire the view.

II

In Search Of...

OK, say you're Saint Peter (play along with me). The Holy Spirit has just descended upon you and your huddling companions, bestowing you with the gift of tongues. As you speak in various languages to the gathering throng, the awed crowd gasps, "How can this be? These people must be drunk."

As Saint Peter, newly named leader of the Church, your answer is:

1. "We've been given the gift of tongues because of divine intervention."

   or

2. "We CAN'T be drunk. It's only 9:00 A.M."

If you chose number 2, you've passed the guy test. Pat yourself on the back (take the pencil out of your hand first). Unable to explain how he and his compatriots—a lowly band of ignorant fishermen—had suddenly become multilingual, Peter knew but one answer: "Well, it's not 'cause we're drunk. We don't start drinking 'til afternoon. So there."

Guys are gifted at short-term answers. Ask them the mileage until their next oil change, the point spread on Sunday's game, or which cable channel carries the "Itsy-Bitsy Bikini Contest," and you'll receive an instant, correct response. Now try a query that's a little more vague—something like "Does this skirt still fit?"—and watch a man's primitive 8-bit computer chip work overtime. (Acceptable answer: "All I know, hon, is that you look great." Unacceptable answers: "The skirt fits, but your hips don't"; "Why not let your breath out and see what breaks?"; and the ever-popular "Were you talking to me? What skirt? You mean the one you're wearing?")

Now let the big boys out of the bag—questions like "Where's this relationship going?" or "What's the meaning of life?"—and watch the Male Mind Meltdown. Palms sweat, the eyes roll back in the head, the tongue sticks to the roof of the mouth. Listen to the long silences punctuated by pauses. It looks like catatonia, only without the drooling.

It's cruel. Really. Men are not built for such questions, but the questions keep coming up. Sure, some of the great philosophers were male, but most of them had too much time on their hands and then went nuts or suicidal or both, and who wants that? I'd rather have beer.

So what follows is the clumsy meandering of a middle-aged male in search of...whatever. Awkward, sometimes bumbling, these offerings are the best I can muster with my eyes rolled back and my tongue permanently affixed to the roof of my mouth.

But, by God, at least I'm not drunk. It's still way too early for that.

Letter Perfect

The females in my family write letters. Mostly business letters and letters to politicians. Correspondence with a purpose.

Their personalities change when aggrieved. My mother, who could charm the snakes back into Ireland, turns into Ma Barker when she's behind the pen. Her style is hard to describe; initially, she sounds like a decent, reasonable person who's merely troubled by a rude sales clerk or the poor performance of her legislator. Then the thumbscrews begin to turn, so tenderly that the readers won't notice until they wake up in an ER somewhere, blood oozing from the stumps of their former digits.

My wife, meanwhile, is far more direct. Unlike my mother, who uses subtlety like a pointillist, Sandee uses irony the way Jackson Pollock uses paint. (Instead of sealing her tomes with wax, my wife uses a Mr. Yuk sticker.) One time, Sandee became frustrated with the local cable television franchise and fired off a hateful letter. "Your company is anal-retentive about receiving payment," my wife observed, "but strangely casual about providing service." The reply from the cable company's president was more insulting than Sandee's original complaint. "You ought to learn," he concluded, "that patience is a virtue." Incensed, my wife sent a copy of the president's letter to the cable syndicate's national headquarters.

Several months later, the president was removed from his job at the local cable company. He was removed because he was promoted.

It's something I've noticed about letter-writing: the result is purely arbitrary. The situation may be resolved, or not. To wit: In the early part of World War II, my grandmother wrote to President Roosevelt, asking that my father, her only son, be excused from the draft. It's hard to imagine what she could have said to convince FDR that her son was somehow the exception, but it worked—she won official dispensation from the Selective Service. No more worries about surprise telegrams ("Greetings from your President...").

So my father enlisted instead.

The Collins females may be insolent on paper, but Collins males are insolent in person.

It's ironic that I, the son and husband of letter-writers, a relative of no fewer than three newspaper reporters, should be such a poor correspondent. (My favored form of communication is electronic mail—abbreviated hiccups that hardly rival the heady arias of a full-blown letter.) But I find myself now a teacher of letters, helping my five-year-old daughter form her first written words.

Faith has trouble with certain letters; she confuses *d* and *b, p* and *q.* And direction poses a problem—she favors writing right to left, Hebrew style. Her preschool teachers assure me it's a phase, a trait common among lefties. So I sit across from my southpaw daughter at the kitchen table, and we draw letters together. We parallel each other in so many ways—her face a smaller, clear-skinned version of my own, her left hand mirroring the movements of my right.

"No, no, sweetie, the hump goes the *other* way."

"Like that?"

"There you go. Nice job!"

I teach writing in a more formal way, too, as a composition instructor at the local university. Once again I'm sitting across a desk, watching younger renditions of myself struggle with the strange song of writing—building an argument, establishing a voice, using irony. (They should learn from my wife.) They even *look* as I did twenty years ago, albeit with baseball caps turned back. Sometimes I write in the margins of their essays, *There you go! Nice job!*

My friend Amy once told me, "I'd give anything

to be a writer like you." I wasn't honored but floored: Amy has a dreamy voice and can play *Amazing Grace* on the bagpipes so well that even atheists cry. What would *I* give for *her* talent? Why would she ever want to trade? What joy could she get out of *d* versus *b, p* versus *q*?

There are diversities of gifts, Saint Paul says, "given to every man to profit withal." I am a somber soldier of my gift. I write because...well, because I can't sing or dance. Whatever talent I have—presumptuous, I know—seems neither an aptitude nor a burden, but part of who I am, as immutable as my height or eye color. It's a living, as Dolly Levi said—some people paint, some sew, I write.

That's *not* what I want to tell my daughter, of course. Faith—my mirror image, the careful crafter of letters—wants to be a ballerina. "You go, girl!" I tell her. Whatever she wants is okay with me. Who can tell where she'll land, *en pointe* or otherwise? Let her dance. One day she'll find where her talents lead. Maybe through college, sitting in a freshman comp section. Maybe to a newspaper. Maybe to parenthood. Make that qarenthoob.

Whatever. The key, I think, is hearing the song, enjoying the letters of the lyric, dancing with whatever talent there is.

"There you go," I'll say to her. "Nice job!"

Hoping Against Hope

I'm sitting in the recliner at two in the morning, watching an infomercial about golf. ("A complete video course for just three easy payments of $19.95.") I can't move because my three-year-old daughter has fallen asleep on my chest. This sleep has been hard-won for Hope, and I'm reluctant to rouse her.

Her labored breathing and coma-like slumber come courtesy of a 102° temperature. It's not the scary kind of fever—I've seen my share of those—just the tail end of a recalcitrant virus. To see my daughter so docile is to see a miracle. Hope is the type of kid whom other parents kindly call "active," meaning she swings from the light fixtures and swings at her sister. But this fever has tamed her. She's so hot she leaves sweat stains on my dark shirt, like Veronica's Veil.

But I'm not thinking about my shirt right now, and I've given up trying to reach for the remote and switch

73

to *anything* but golf. ("Thanks to your video golf series, I've shaved eight strokes from my score. In fact,
I've left my wife and kids to join the pro tour...") I'm
thinking, instead, about this article, the one you're
reading now. I'm thinking that one day Hope and her
sister will be old enough to read it, and how embar-
rassed I'll be when they discover this public admission
by their old man:

When my kids are sick, I'm sorry I had kids at all.

Don't get me wrong—it's not for the obvious, selfish reasons. (Well, not entirely.) It's not the lost sleep.
It's not the agile dance around projectile vomiting at
4:00 A.M. It's not the lost work days taken as sick days
when I was, in fact, never sick. It's not the piled-up
laundry, grown higher and ranker each day because
you can't leave your kid long enough to turn on the
washer. It's not the protracted negotiations with one's
spouse about who's turn it is to do what. It's not the
feeling of imprisonment, stuck inside this petri dish of
disease while outside the sun is shining (but you know
that bundling up your sick child for even a short re-
spite in the fresh air will take at least thirty minutes of
boots, coats, and scarves, plus fifteen minutes to find
two mittens that aren't encrusted with snot). It's not
the endless variations on the BRAT diet—bananas, rice,
applesauce, and toast. It's not even the sheer drudgery
of sickness.

It's moments like this, in a recliner at 2:00 A.M.,
waiting, waiting, waiting for a child's fever to break,

waiting for her rapid, shallow breathing to ease, count-ing the seconds between coughing fits to see if the medi-cine is working, leaving phone messages on the doctor's answering machine, begging for a better antibiotic. It's deep into nights like this, amid the smell of VapoRub and sweat, that I realize a mistake has been made, that I'm not cut out for this. In a rare case of divine over-sight, God picked the wrong guy for the job.

You'd think—as you conjure up this picture of me in Perfect Parental Posture, nursing a sick child on my own chest—you'd think that I'd feel competent and confident. I feel anything but. Although nothing pre-pared me for the slings and arrows of parenthood, I've adjusted to most of it—the mad shifts in scheduling, the Herculean tasks of daily living. Oh, it's exasperat-ing and sometimes irritating, but it's also spontaneous and fun.

Until now. Until nights like this, when I'm rendered helplessly impotent, when I can do nothing but wait.

I am an American male. I change my own oil. I do my own taxes. I vote my own conscience. And I never, ever call the repairman. To just sit here and wait and wait and...where's the owner's manual? What prob-lem is this that I cannot solve, this calculus of illness? I am dyslexic in this new math, a frustrated student. Just give me a pair of needle-nose pliers, a wiring dia-gram and some duct tape, and I'll...

I'll do nothing. Do nothing but wait. So that's what I'll do. Because, I'm learning, it's all I *can* do. Hold her here, spoon in some Tylenol, occasionally wipe her brow. That's it. Wait.

By sundown tomorrow, my wife assures me, Hope will be back to her old self—a mixed blessing, by most accounts. But I will silently cheer her whining then, happy, at least for a moment, that she and I have survived this siege. We'll both live a little longer to learn more about each other.

I've learned, for instance, practically all there is to know about golf—about taking your time, about playing the lie, about reckoning the doglegs and occasional hazards. And when my daughter is old enough to read, she'll learn the metaphoric possibilities of her own name. She'll learn how Hope can teach patience, even to the most reluctant of students.

The Wedding at Cana

It's a cliché I cannot abide: You always hurt the ones you love. But why? Just because they're close by? Because you can? Because you know their weak spot? Because no one else would put up with such behavior? (Try this simple test: Go to your boss and say, "I'm still smarting from that crack you made about my weight three years ago. You should be ashamed of yourself." Your boss will either [a] call security; [b] recommend that you take advantage of the company's abundant mental-health benefits; or [c] both. Now try the same remark on your spouse. Chances are your spouse won't bat an eye or, more likely, will launch an equally cruel counterattack.)

I have watched my hair turn gray. I've felt my body slowly betray me—little hurts that are slow to heal, arthritis in my big toe, a trick knee. But nothing has been as horrific as watching myself turn on those I love—my wife, my kids, my friends. It's like rubber-necking at a traffic accident: you can't believe that you, too, are engaging in this behavior. You don't want to do it, but you do it anyhow.

I have exploded with the swiftness of a terrorist grenade, sending young children scattering to their rooms ahead of the verbal shrapnel. I have chased rude drivers for three miles on the highway, just to yell at them for cutting me off in the previous zip code. They laugh at me and speed away. Can you blame them? I recently confronted a store clerk for shortchanging me by thirty-five cents. Did I really suspect her of stealing? Did I think she carefully plotted her strategy? "Let's see, thirty-five cents here, thirty-five cents there, and pretty soon I'll have...*seventy cents!*"

I have seen the best minds of my generation say cruel, humiliating things to the people they love most. Two friends of mine—longtime lovers—had the following conversation:

> *Partner #1:* I have one thing to say to you: Sweeping your hair over that bald spot isn't working anymore.
> *Partner #2:* I have one *word* to say to you: Liposuction!

They didn't speak to each other for days. Ten years in a committed relationship and *this* is the level of discourse? We—or should I say *I?*—can forget in an instant the countless kindnesses experienced each day, but we will *never* forget the slightest slight. I can successfully nurse any small sore into a big, festering wound. It's a challenge, but I can do it.

If we're going to engage in such behavior, then why not go all the way and settle our scores like eight-year-olds? Why don't we rub our knuckles *hard* into each other's scalp until someone yells, "Uncle"? Or hold our breath until we turn blue?

What is *wrong* with us, anyway?

I have this theory about heaven. If you get past Saint Peter—Checkpoint Charlie—you get to meet God. But because this is heaven—everything you ever wanted—you also get to quiz God. You get to ask all the hard questions: Where's my baseball glove from eighth grade? What's the story with Hitler? And why don't you like the Cubs?

In return, God gets to ask *you* questions. I'm sure there are things we do that totally mystify the Almighty. Why are you so petty with one another? What made you think asparagus was edible? And, the Big One: Who said marriage was a good idea?

"But you made it a *sacrament!*" you'll bluster.

"Sure," God may well respond, "and I made Extreme Unction a sacrament. Does that mean I want everyone to die? My own son didn't marry."

"But the wedding at Cana..."

"Where everyone panicked because they just *had* to keep drinking? Buy a clue. It's not for everyone.

Remember Adam and Eve? Talk about dysfunctional. First thing that goes wrong, and what happens? They fight, they lie, they blame each other. And here I got them a nice toaster for a wedding gift. I shoulda known then."

OK, I jest. But not by much. At what point in our civilization did we say, "Let's put these two people in the same room for the next fifty years and see what happens...." And each succeeding generation examines the results and says, "Hey! What a bad idea! Let's do it again!"

I'm speaking to you as a happily married man. I love my wife, faults and all. I am eternally grateful for her patience. Sandee is brave in the face of my remarkable sins, and I cannot tell you why. I can't imagine my life without her.

But.

But.

But but. But what I've seen people do to each other in the name of marriage. What I've done myself. I sit here, in this chair, fingers clicking across the keyboard, wondering what chaotic fate threw my wife and me together fifteen years ago. The joy has been inexplicable. The pain I wouldn't wish on my worst enemy.

This is a *sacrament?*

When I was young, I saw divorce as a failing—it was his fault, it was her fault, it was their fault. Now I'm older, the witness to three billion divorces, and I can give you no reason. Friends of mine—intelligent, fair-minded, kind, compassionate—have called it quits, and I can't say why. Some are happier. Some aren't. It terrifies me. Will Sandee wake up one fine day, feel my sleepy breath on her neck, spy yesterday's jeans hanging on the bedpost, and suddenly understand that she must get out, and now? Will I?

Marriage is a sacrament because it requires prayer. It requires God. It requires a legion of angels—saviors, like cavalry. Like Calvary.

Speaking of Saint Peter: My friend Danny called from Boston to tell me his father had died.

"I didn't know he was sick," I said.

"All his life," Danny replied. "So it was time." He talked about his dad and how, several years ago, they had finally made their peace. "Those last few years he was alive," Danny said, "we could finally talk, eye-to-eye, because we knew that I might never see him again."

"What a wonderful story," I said, and I held that thought in my heart until another friend told me the truth: Danny's father had killed himself.

For a moment I felt betrayed: Why had Dan lied to me? I thought we were friends. He must be devastated by this sudden, explosive end.

Not at all, it turns out. Danny knew his father, knew what he was capable of. That's what he meant: at any moment he might never see his father again. As a teenager, Danny later told me, he had felt abandoned by his father, who stood not three feet away but may as well have been back in Ireland. Cursed by Irish reticence, his father never once hugged his son, and kissed Danny good night only when he was drunk, which was quite often. But rather than buy into this Gaelic cliché, Danny fought back. Rather than finding solace in 100-proof anger, Danny spoke to his father. Danny cried in front of his father. Danny beat back the demons of his own history, fists flailing, tears falling. When his dad turned on the ignition in that closed garage, Danny's prayers were with him. I doubt if he died a happy man, but he died as the father of a loving child, and few of us can hope for much more. If Saint Peter awaited him at the Pearly Gates, I hope he was as impressed as I was with that small miracle. God and Danny's dad can pour themselves a nice Stout and quiz each other all night long.

This is my love song to all who have withstood my misplaced wrath. This is my *mea culpa* for untold misunderstandings, unrequited anger, unspoken pain. I have been given vast gifts in the form of a wife and children, in the form of friends, family, lovers, coworkers, but like a selfish child at Christmas, I have chosen instead to complain about the color of this generous present, or notice only the price tag that's left there by accident.

No more. No more barbarity on the parkway, one finger out the window. No more swearing at children under seven. This is another sacrament you're witnessing, the sacrament of reconciliation. If I cannot divine the *mysterium tremendum* of love, life, the universe, and the Cubs, I can at least put out my open hand, an offering of penance for my imperfect marriage, my imperfect past, my imperfect self, my uncertain future, my unknowable God. This is a kinder, gentler Mark speaking to you, a New Year's Resolute Mark.

My resolutions may sound ambitious, but they're not forever—they're just for today.

Or for an *hour,* if I'm driving.

Forgiveness

Last week I took my five-year-old, Faith, to the bus stop for her first day of kindergarten. We had the typical tears and quaking sobs, but then Faith told me to straighten up because I was embarrassing her. So I snuffled up my snot and let her get on the bus.

The other parents offered hankies and sympathy. Then the conversation turned to "how tough it is to raise kids these days"—a popular topic among young moms and dads. And God knows I didn't argue: I needed the validation that I'm not crazy, that other people struggle with sleeplessness and worry and stretched finances. Sometimes my wife and I rent a video to relax, and we'll fall asleep before the FBI warning is half over.

But this idea about "nowadays"—that parenting used to be easier, somehow. That we've got it tougher than *our* parents had it.

Ummm....no. Not nearly. Not by a long shot.

It's true that we probably won't enjoy the same level of financial achievement our parents enjoyed. It's also true that our kids face unique challenges—weapons in the schools, a sex life that starts around...I dunno, fourth grade. But this notion that parents today are suffering like those of no other generation... puh-LEEZE.

The comparisons usually run like this:

1. "I try to spend as much time at home with the kids. My father just wasn't there for me...." That's true—it was called "working for a living." Maybe he was spending your milk money at the track, but chances are he was in the mill, slaving over an open hearth so you could go to school or get your teeth fixed on his union dental plan. Or he was struggling at a corporate job that really *owned* him; his generation believed in company loyalty. OK, so he was naive. Is that his fault?

2. "My mother could afford to stay home...." Of course, your mother's career options were hamstrung by her gender. Equal opportunities for women didn't just happen. Women like your mom, perhaps, put up a stink, and now our diverse work force sings in a higher key.

Then again, maybe your parents thought it was *cheaper* if your mom stayed home to cook meals, to run errands, to keep the house together—the same things you now *pay* someone else to do. And maybe your mom was lucky enough to have both a rewarding career and a family—the very same things you're after, only she complained a *lot* less than you do.

3. "I have to drive my kids everywhere—to soccer practice, dance rehearsal, the pool...." Whoa, pal, who agreed to that schedule? You did. Or are you complaining because your kids have opportunities you didn't have—you're *sorry* about that?

Like most forms of whining, these petty complaints (OK, *my* petty complaints) have a deeper, more troubling root. We, the children of '50s parents, are ticked because Ozzie came home happy from his nice job exactly at six and Harriet wore pearls while vacuuming their sixteen-bedroom house...meanwhile, *our* parents stitched the pockets of hand-me-down jeans and drank Schlitz from whatever glass was clean.

Bulletin: The '50s weren't a television show. They were hard work and bomb shelters and black folk on the back of the bus. Ozzie and Harriet were fiction, about as real as a letter to *Penthouse*.

Our complaints are meant to ease our guilt. We remember our parents as often tired, often distant, or rarely home—but *we* work just as hard and have to deal with the same regret: trading money for love. They, like us, tried their best. Sure, some parents drank. Some were lazy. Some were even abusive. Some were wonderful. And we're *no* different.

Blame simply won't work. There's no one to blame. Slings and arrows can pierce a childhood, and I'm really sorry about that, but searching out the guilty party two decades later just won't help.

Instead, it's about forgiveness, about forgiving everybody. (Which doesn't mean "forgive and forget." *No one* forgets.) If you really want to save your children from this relentless cycle of growing up feeling both guilty and victimized, then that means coming clean: We've become our parents, as frightening as that is to hear. We've inherited some version of their divine eccentricity, their flawed affection. Though we disguise our foibles with nomenclature ("weird" is now "dysfunctional"), a ruse by any other name still smells.

Maybe forgiving your parents their humanity is the first step in forgiving yourself. Correction: forgiving *myself*. In Faith's five short years, I've let her down a million times. (That's 550 times a day.) The only penance I can offer is this essay, my *mea culpa* to her and her siblings when they're all old enough to read. To be a parent means to forever second-guess yourself, so much so that you forget what you've done right.

And my wife and I must've done something right, because Faith came back from her first day of school full of laughter and stories, eyes bright with excitement, clutching the flower she had drawn just for me, running down the driveway into my waiting arms, her tiny hands circling my torso, and I swear to you there is a merciful, loving God because nothing else can explain such glorious math.

And the first thing I did then? Called Mom and Dad. They were anxious to know how it went.

"Great," I told them. "Everything turned out great."

I'm Going to Disney World! Where's My Gun?

A few years back, on Father's Day, my oldest daughter gave me a plaster cast of her hand. "I made this for you, Daddy," four-year-old Faith said. "It's a statue of my hand." As paternal tears welled in my eyes, Faith added: "It's a statue of my hand reaching for the purple Jasmine at Toys 'R Us."

Yes. Well. So much for sentiment. What seemed like a touching moment was just another of Faith's ruses to buy all things Disney. My three children—now ages six, four, and six months—are firmly ensconced on the Disney marketing juggernaut. If it were up to Faith, we'd even buy Uncle Walt's cryto-crypt, the Tomb of the Cold Cartoonist. (Many are drawn, but few are frozen.)

So it was with great interest that I've been following the Southern Baptists' decision to boycott Disney and its subsidiaries (which includes the Anaheim Mighty Ducks, the Anaheim Angels, the state of California, ABC, ESPN, LBJ, R&R, Touchstone Pictures, Hollywood Records, the Iberian Peninsula, the color yellow, cirrus clouds, most prepositions, and the '50s, plus copyright royalties on all people nicknamed Mickey). I mean, good *luck*. It's like boycotting sunlight.

But it wasn't for the same reasons that I've grown to despise the Florida rat. The Southern Baptists are upset about Disney's outrageous employment policies, which insist on treating people equally, and you know where *that* will lead. Trouble. Right here in Disney World. With a capital *D* and that rhymes with *P* and that stands for pool. Or prejudice. Or something.

No, I'm upset because my daughters are square-eyed from watching so many Disney videos. ("Where are the kids?" I ask my wife. "You mean Walt's junkies?" my wife responds, pointing to the television.) Now before you cast any aspersions (which, by the way, are 40 percent Disney-owned), let me say this: we limit our kids' television intake—two hours a day, usually less. But every Disney flick features an ad for three *other* Disney movies, so that's what the kids ask for on their birthdays. We've built quite a collection.

A disturbing collection, if you ask me.

Virtually every Disney plot features some NC-17 version of dysfunctional parenting. We've got evil stepmothers (*Cinderella, Snow White*), evil guardians (*Hunchback of Notre Dame*), bumbling, foolish fathers (*Beauty and the Beast, Aladdin*), totally AWOL fathers/mothers (*Aladdin, Dumbo*), and fathers who are so backward they're downright mean (*The Little Mermaid, Peter Pan, Mary Poppins*). There are two exceptions: Simba's parents seem healthy and happy in *The Lion King*...until Simba's dad buys the veldt, right there in front of horrified eyes (a scene akin to what we see in that famous Disney snuff film, *Bambi,* in which the main character's mother eats a fatal feast of lead. Move over, Arnold, we're talking QUALITY FAMILY ENTERTAINMENT). And Pocahontas' dad seems nice, in a warrior-king kind of way.

But *Pocahontas* raises all sorts of other problems, especially for me, the father of three little girls. For those of you unfamiliar with the movie (which is 100 percent historically accurate, up until the opening credits), Pocahontas is the young daughter of an American Indian who partners with that famous English softy, John Smith, to avert war between the adventurers and the invaded. I'm not worried that my daughters will mistake this for actual history; I'm concerned that they'll think such a Hollywood ending is really possible. I'm worried that they'll think that collisions between cultures can be controlled through the love of a teenager for an older man. I'm worried that Pocahontas might seem...*real*. Pocahontas of the impossible waistline. Pocahontas, faultless speaker of the King's English. Pocahontas, whose hair, as my friend Kristi observed, should have received top billing. Pocahontas, who could speak to animals and trees. Pocahontas of the amazing bosom, her size-8 body poured into an off-the-shoulder size-6 buckskin dress.

Pocahontas the Everything. A Native American Joan of Arc with the body of a Playboy bunny. An environmentalist Playboy bunny who's bilingual.

When my third daughter was born, an attending doctor turned to me and said, "You were probably hoping for a boy." I couldn't be happier with three girls. (Three boys would've been fine, too. Less destructive, I'll bet.) And it's an amazing time to be a woman. Barriers are dropping everyday. Women's pro basketball. Women in politics. Women in newsrooms. Women in science. Never enough, but growing.

Still, each opportunity means added pressure—pressure to be everything, and to be sexy too. Attitudes don't change overnight. Some of the most egregious sexists I've met have been younger than I. In the future I will screen each of my daughters' gentleman callers: *Please fill out the following questionnaire. #1: Do you respect woman as you do men? #2: Do you know that your date's father owns a shoulder-launched, heat-seeking Sidewinder missile? Be back by 10:00 P.M. Enjoy yourself.*

My wife is a skilled religion instructor. When she tells stories to our kids, Sandee emphasizes the biblical stories of strong women. Those are my favorites, too.

When Abraham's wife, Sarah, is told that she will have a child after years of being barren, she laughs derisively.

Imagine! Laughing at God!

Sarah doesn't care. Like most older women, she's heard promises before. Oh, she'll prove her faith soon enough—she'll let Abraham take her beloved Isaac to the mountain, a knife hidden near the sacrificial altar—but it won't be faith without comment. I say good for Sarah. And Ruth the Moabite will stay with her widowed mother-in-law, scraping up the discarded grain in a barley field in Bethlehem. And centuries later, from Ruth's lineage, another young woman will travel to Bethlehem to settle another promise, another seed planted and plucked—fruit for another sacrifice, another offering, another faith, another life.

This is what I want to tell my daughters about heroines. They don't have sixteen-inch waistlines. They come from all sorts of families. Their hair isn't important. They laugh at God. They pray to God. They stick by their people. They love hard, but they know it won't cure everything. They make mistakes. They listen to their hearts. They make choices. They feed others. They raise children as best they know, without ever fully knowing. There are men in their lives, and those men are important, but most of them are not the Second Coming, no matter what they might tell you.

It's the best I can offer: a sermon. I have been given these three magical women—Faith, Hope, and Grace, my own manna from heaven, everything I could ask for—only to send them away one day like all good parents, send them into the world armed with advice, clean underwear, a $20 bill snuck into their pockets.

It's all I can do. What more is left?

Shalom, my daughters. Next year in Jerusalem.

Doesn't Anybody Stay in One Place Anymore?

I grew up in Forest Hills, which you may or may not know is a suburb of Pittsburgh. That's not exactly true. Although the neighborhood was loyal to the Pirates and the Steelers (which, in my early youth, was a true act of faith), and although we had a city-bound streetcar right down the middle of Ardmore Boulevard, we were more closely allied with the Turtle Creek Valley. Even our telephone exchanges began with VAlley-3 or VAlley-4.

It's no wonder. Virtually every father on our street was a present or former employee of the Westinghouse plant on Electric Avenue in East Pittsburgh/Turtle Creek. ("Father" and "wage-earner" were synonymous back then.) Many had moved up the hill from Pitcairn, Wilmerding, Wall—the mill towns in the hollow. In grade school, when Sister Marie asked where our fathers worked, we found that the family revenue stream for our entire grade could be reduced to three choices: Westinghouse, United States Steel's Edgar Thomson Works, and Other. It was a demographic profile played out all around the county: Homestead, Hazelwood, Braddock, Millvale.

My memories are visceral, too. I remember hearing the American cars roar to life each morning, accompanied by the occasional four-letter sonata. Three times each day our quiet street had something of a rush hour, as the night crews and day crews and those who manned the swing shift passed one another with a nod and a wave. And I remember one adolescent summer when I filled in a few mornings for a friend who sold the morning paper at the mouth of the cavernous Westinghouse plant. The *Pittsburgh Post-Gazette* cost fifteen cents then; I learned how to grab a proffered quarter, fold a paper, and squeeze the dime change into each callused hand in under three seconds. I *had* to be efficient: the stream of incoming proletariat seemed endless. And I remember summer evenings when I was a batboy for the Westinghouse softball leagues that played at the company's recreation center at the top of our street. Two fields, two games a night, four months a year. Everyone had uniforms. And the stands were packed.

And then, suddenly, it was gone.

Well, it took a few years, but it seemed the blink of an eye. It started with some talk of layoffs in the mid-'70s or so, then the furloughs became longer, till finally it just all dwindled away—not with a bang, but a whimper. By the time the plant officially closed in 1988, only a few hundred workers were left. Many of the folks in our neighborhood either took early retirements or other jobs until they could collect their pensions. Some never fully recovered.

By the late '70s/early '80s, Westinghouse's layoffs were just a tiny ripple in the avalanche of bleak economic news that buffeted Pittsburgh. We found we weren't alone. Across the region, plant after plant was shutting down; our troubles seemed dwarfed by those in the Mon Valley and Aliquippa and Johnstown. (While we weren't marching with radical priests or protesting outside of USX, we knew what led folks to do just that.)

What's happened since then is a debate you've heard before. Depending on who you talk to, Pittsburgh either "recovered," thanks to the two-pronged influx of high-tech and healthcare jobs, or it has "limped along" as displaced workers learned to live on lower-wage, service-sector jobs. It's a passionate debate, and your position depends squarely on how you've fared during the past fifteen years: as someone who landed in viable industry, or as a casualty of the collision of economic forces far beyond your control.

But there was another effect as well, one that transcends generations. My thirtysomething compatriots and I learned an unspoken lesson from that early trauma: Trust no one. Keep on your toes so you know when to jump. While our fathers had toiled under the illusion of lifetime positions, protected (we thought) by unions and a good dental plan, we learned quickly to fend for ourselves. Despite the rosy reassurances of well-meaning executives, we learned that higher-ups in corporate headquarters in faraway cities make all of the real decisions.

It's not just our parents' ordeal that has made us suspicious. I have friends who've worked in banking and computer firms and newspapers and, most recently, in the venerable healthcare industry, and many have found out firsthand the capricious nature of employment. Restructurings, "right-sizings," and reorganizations have left many behind, clutching pink slips and want ads. And these aren't blue-collar jobs, but college-trained professionals whose parents sent them to school in the (vain) hope that their lot in life would be more secure.

We've learned to be as loyal to the company as the company is to us. We craft our own careers as best we can, no longer expecting a promotion or even long-term employment, and feeling no remorse for leaving a job after one or two years, taking with us the training, the business contacts, the experience. We've become conversant about portable IRAs and Keoughs and other self-run pension plans, knowing as the workers at LTV Steel discovered a decade ago that even a company's retirement monies aren't sacred. It's both selfish and practical; we feel as rootless as our resumes, jumping from job to job, never developing the kind of relationships that…well, that lead you to play softball with your coworkers on warm summer evenings. But we dare not be lulled into loyalty or let another job opportunity slip by, knowing too well that we're a heartbeat away from the unemployment office. ("Please keep behind the yellow line until your name is called…")

Such self-reliance might seem praiseworthy: young professionals adapting to a changing economy. But there's a price to be paid for the footloose, both for the company and the worker. Corporations often complain about the cost of rapid turnover yet cannot see how layoffs in one division make folks in the other divisions a tad nervous. And me and my adaptable friends might never witness the sense of community that builds among workers who labor shoulder-to-shoulder for twenty-odd years. Many of us don't know what it's like to down a few beers at the company picnic, or to invite one hundred coworkers to your daughter's wedding, or to feel the pride of working with one's hands to make something other than a memo, or to get teary-eyed at Stash's retirement party. ("Retiring" for us will simply mean no more cover letters. We don't expect a gold watch; we hardly expect the Social Security system to be viable.)

The new company motto is "lean and mean." "Personnel" departments (which sounded too close to "personal") have given over to "Human Resources"—a coldly ironic title only Marx could appreciate. We've gone from the cradle-to-grave company to pay-as-you-go healthcare and entire departments staffed by temps. While we fret about the economic encroachments of the Japanese and the Germans and now the Chinese, we forget that we're still the most productive country on the planet, mostly because we know how to work and work well and work together. It's an innate, uniquely American capacity that Hitler fatally miscalculated. It's the same trait that built this entire town, this entire country. Time was when Polish-Americans and Slovak-Americans and African-Americans and Italian-Americans and Irish-Americans hunkered down into the hearths to sweat out huge slabs of steel that fueled the economic engine of a nation. Now here we are, the grandsons and granddaughters of those immigrants, circling the want ads for the next job, circling the wagons of our own economic future, relying on our wits and quick feet to get by, to secure some kind of future for the next generation.

Like our parents and our grandparents before us, we're doing what we have to do to survive. But something seems missing. Maybe the mill town camaraderie was forced, but it looks awfully attractive in the rearview mirror.

Last summer I drove past the Westinghouse soft-ball fields near my parents' house. They were playing again—not nearly as many teams, and probably more ringers, but that's not important. Growing up, it seemed like just a game. Now I realize what it takes to play, how much preparation, how hard you have to work just to play .500 ball, just to break even.

Wearing the Genes
in My Family

If you've ever looked underneath the body of a '60s sports car, chances are you'll see a dual-exhaust system shaped like a Y. It matches the male Y chromosome. Men are genetically built to lust after '60s muscle cars in the same way...well, in the same way they lust for muscles after turning sixty.

At my age, I don't even *drive* sixty. My idea of car renovation is changing the oil. My idea of adventure is changing lanes.

But when I spy an old GTO or Barracuda or Javelin pulling beside me at a red light, my heart goes all aflutter. In my fantasies, I'm rebuilding a '69 Firebird, using nothing more than a can of starting fluid, a half-inch open-end wrench (none of that prissy metric stuff), and a radio that plays only Roy Orbison. Suddenly,

I'm transformed from the Writer Formerly Known as Mark to a guy in mechanic's overalls, wiping my hands on an orange rag, and my name, Buzz (or maybe Speed), stitched in red over my heart. I smoke Luckies. Suddenly, gas is cheap again, and so's my eight-track tape player. My license plate reads 2BAD4U or 8MYDUST. I regularly outrun the police, who have a begrudging respect for me and my machine. Women leave love notes in lipstick on my windshield.

I wake from my dream because the guy behind me is beeping. The light has turned green. I ease my mini-van into gear, careful not to spill my travel mug of decaf.

My father drove a minivan, too, except they weren't called that in the '60s. It was a VW microbus, and he wasn't a hippie. He was a dad.

I've become a father, too. I don't just mean "I have kids"—not that kind of fatherhood. I mean I have *become my father*. Had you told me this twenty years ago, back when my hair was long and my tolerance short, back when my father was the squarest thing on planet Earth, I would've laughed so hard I'd have spit up my illicit beer. "No, no, no," my seventeen-year-old self would've told you, "I'll *never* be like my dad."

Well, I'm not just *like* my dad, I *am* my dad. OK, I'm a few decades younger, have a goatee, and vote Democrat, but other than that we may as well be clones. The other night I caught my reflection in the kitchen window: I was sitting on the back porch, drinking a beer, bitching about the body work I needed to do on the van. If you change the beer from Rolling Rock to Old German and change the van from a Chrysler to a VW, then it could be 1968, and I could be my old man. Deja vu all over again.

Often, like him, I'll fetch the morning paper still in my jammies. (How it got in my jammies I'll never know.) I spend weekends unshaven. I often eat my lunch at my desk—leftovers out of a Tupperware container. I'm rude to phone solicitors. ("Oh, you want *Mark* Collins. Sorry, he's not here. In fact, he died. Don't bother calling back, 'cause I'll still be dead.") And, *just* like my Dad, I take it personally when my favorite sports team loses, often venting my frustration at the television itself: "Well, there's another afternoon of my life wasted," I hiss at the set as I slam it off. "Thanks, guys. By the way, if you see my heart out there, just go ahead an' stomp it flat. I won't be needing it anymore."

When does all this happen? At what point do young men trip into somewhat older men, becoming various incarnations of their fathers? At what point do we trade our sedans for station wagons and minivans and start drinking decaf? I don't remember passing a signpost; one day I woke up, looked in the mirror, and saw my father wearing a goatee. (I had two thoughts: First, what's my father doing in the mirror? Second, he oughta *shave* that thing. Looks like a caterpillar crawled around his mouth and died.)

Truth is, I don't mind being my father. It's a shock, but it's not bad. What's weird is wondering how I got from there to here; when, as Jackson Browne asked, did that road turn onto the one I'm on?

I have one guess. For me, it happened on a morning in May a few years back, when my oldest daughter was born and I really did become a dad. I was in the operating room when my wife delivered, and I was the first to hold Faith (after, of course, the nurse, who cleaned her up so she didn't look like an outtake from *Night of the Living Dead*). And I remember holding this crying, wrinkled, smelly mass of protoplasm, thinking, *I know they keep saying this is my kid, but surely there's a mistake. I've never met this person before in my life. Believe me, I'd remember.*

And the first thing I said to my new daughter?

"Hello, Faith Margaret. I'm your dad. I love you."

Now where did *that* come from?

I have this vision: My kids will be on a shrink's couch many years hence, and the therapist will ask, "So what do you remember about your father?" And they'll think for a minute, then reply, "His neck. The bottom of his chin. He was always looking up."

This is true. When I'm exasperated (like always), I look toward the ceiling, sometimes bringing my hand to my forehead like Homer Simpson. (*Doh!*) I'm not sure why—am I looking to heaven for guidance? Do I expect the answer to my distress to be written in the stars?

Actually, I know why I do it: my father did it. When my brother and sister and I would engage in something particularly repugnant—punching each other, setting something on fire, or (the BIG ONE), borrowing one of Dad's tools for emergency surgery on the Philco hi-fi (which wasn't even *broken!* Isn't that *funny!*)—he'd stare skyward and stagger back a few paces, as if he'd just witnessed the Rapture, and it wasn't quite what he'd expected. Then he'd close his eyes and count, silently, to himself, until he could talk calmly to us, albeit through gritted teeth. We just stood there while he counted, waiting out his urge to commit mayhem. Once I think he counted to a million and three.

When I see old college buddies—folks I haven't seen since Carter was president—I want to tell them, "I'm not the person you see before you. I cannot explain how I am different, but I'm a father now, and it has changed everything." It's as if I've had plastic surgery or I've grown a third foot or I speak only Swahili.

Which makes me wonder about *my* father. What was he like before he was exasperated by us? I hear stories of his days in the Navy, or his time in college, and they seem like stories from another planet. When, at the age of twenty, my father was told that only officers were allowed to go on shore leave, he asked a chief petty officer if he could borrow his uniform. The CPO, half-asleep, looked at my father, smiled, and said sure. So my father put on the sleeping man's uniform and tried to leave the ship.

His plan would've gone perfectly, had the uniform fit perfectly. As it was, the CPO's pants dragged on the ground, and his jacket overwhelmed my dad's five-foot-ten-inch frame. The real giveaway to the MP on duty was the four stripes on the sleeve, denoting sixteen years of naval service.

When I first heard this story, it was *my* turn to be exasperated. "What did they do to you?" I asked.

"Gave me a lecture," my dad said. "They really yelled at the poor guy who lent me the uniform."

"Um, isn't impersonating an officer a serious offense?" I asked.

My father thought a minute. "I guess so," he said. This had never occurred to him.

I know why: on the scale of sins committed during World War II, this was a venial offense. There are still things about the war my father cannot discuss, fifty years after the fact. I've seen this scene played out at half a dozen Irish wakes: men deal with grief by not talking about it. Whole books have been written on this very subject, urging men to talk about their feelings. These books were written by people who never waited by an airstrip for a buddy who would never return. Even after countless sessions on the shrink's couch, I cannot say that talking about grief and loss makes them manageable. I do know this: If you're swimming to keep from drowning, no one should criticize your stroke.

In Scotland they've cloned a sheep, putting the cell of one ewe into the egg of another, then planting the fertilized egg into a third ewe.

Theoretically, at least, men aren't really necessary anymore to propagate the species. Many women will cheer this advance, and who can blame them?

This essay is about genes. I carry with me the storehouse of a thousand generations, a history of Irish and German and French and Indian blood, all of it tragically, comically human.

This is a story of religion, and of doubt. God could've chosen an easier species to deal with; dolphins are more loving, loyal, and obedient and have way more fun. God could've chosen less complicated messengers than men like Moses and Allah, whose followers—disciples of the same God—still fight to the death. And what kind of Divine Parent would send Jesus into the world to preach the creed of love and redemption and the meek inheriting the earth, knowing, *knowing,* the grievous three hours at Calvary? This is the same God who sent me my three wondrous children?

On this my faith rests: I am called to be human, as close to divine as I can, fully aware that I'm embarking on a journey whose goal surpasses all understanding. For my father's sake, for my children's sake, and for the sake of a thousand generations before and hence, I am ordered to go against my wretched nature, to find a way to live that lets all of us live, to rise up against the selfish temper of my genetic code and overcome its savage, prewired knack for blood.

In the caves of Europe, ancient spears have been found, carved by prehominids whose very survival depended on the death caused by weapons such as these. Humankind, always the toolmaker, still builds machines today—machines that harvest food, machines that look good at red lights, machines that safely haul children to soccer games, machines that save lives, machines that take lives, machines that rip the flesh off another human at a thousand paces. My father, a civil engineer trained on the GI Bill, helped to design the first deep-space antenna, used to track the Apollo missions to the moon. Imagine that. And while I haven't inherited his skill, I *can* change the disc brakes on a man-made Chevy, albeit while taking God's name in vain. I can name most of the tools in the Craftsman catalog. I can fix nearly all of my daughters' toys. With these hands and brain, I can make a difference...

...if only I knew how. I have no owner's manual, just this flawed but precisely detailed genetic blueprint, the inscrutable, screwed-up, double-edged helix I see in my father's face, the faces of my children, the face in the mirror still waiting for my answer.

Kids 'n Cars, Part Two

L ast Saturday we had to put our cat, Mookie Wilson, to sleep. She was a character. Rescued from the streets, Mookie was a great mouser but a lousy bedtime companion and none too accurate with the litter box. Then last week, she decided to hide behind the washer and wait for death.

I cried when I left Mookie at the vet's for the last time, but not for the expected reasons. I had already made me peace with Mooks, all the way to the hospital. Now I was crying because of something the vet had said: "An outdoor cat like Mookie—well, twelve years is a ripe age."

"You mean they usually die of feline leukemia or rabies or something?" I asked.

"Well, those things, of course," the vet replied, "but mostly it's cars."

So I was crying not because of what I had lost, but what I could lose, because I was scared. I was thinking of my kids, who won't be driving for another ten years.

I don't frighten easily. I've shot the rapids, played hockey without a helmet, had dinner with my in-laws. But two tons of metal spinning out of control is not a game or a kick or a thrill. It's blood and broken bones and mass cards and regret.

I know. In college I worked part-time collecting blood samples at a local hospital. After a couple years I got some seniority so I could pick my floor. "Anything but the rehab floor," I told them. "Anything but that." I had simply seen too much. Too many head traumas, young patients wearing their bandages like turbans, staring back at me, their vacant eyes unmoored, adrift. The pins in their legs could repair their broken bones but not their broken families, and so much of it because of high-octane cars fueled by higher-proof alcohol. The ER nurses had seen so many motor vehicle accidents they called them "donor vehicle accidents," because so many head cases ended up dead, giving over their organs to some lucky recipient.

I hope their families got some solace out of that gift. I hope.

And those were the memories I had outside the vet's office. I was thinking of all I need to tell my little girls. I was thinking how invincible I felt when *I* was sixteen, and drove like it—how the grace of God and good brakes had saved my life at least a dozen times.

My mother, schooled in the Baltimore Catechism, used to touch my teenaged shoulder before I drove off. "Let the Infant Jesus put his hands on the steering wheel," she'd tell me. My brother, who turned white-lipped and fearful when I was driving, said that the Infant Jesus must've never had a license.

So here I was, many years later, crying in the parking lot of a vet's office because I knew one day I would let my daughters leave, keys in hand. In my mind's eye I can see them, ten years hence: makeup, earrings, stylish clothes that seem (to me) too saucy. They'll be headed to school or maybe a basketball game. They'll get in the car, turn on the radio loud. They'll drive safely until they're out of sight, and I'll wave to them, trying desperately to breathe around the heart now lodged in my throat, wondering if I had told them enough, wondering if they would learn the way I learned, wondering if it was too late.

A Memorial for
the Rest of Us

With the opening of the Holocaust Memorial in Washington, D.C., it was inevitable that other wronged ethnic groups would call for their own museum. On the electronic bulletin board to which I subscribe, one writer noted that Native Americans had suffered their own genocidal episodes, either starved to death or forced to march or just plain massacred. Unlike the Holocaust, the writer said, Americans were directly responsible for the decimation of an indigenous race, a race that peopled this very continent.

Which is entirely true, and entirely beside the point.

What's surprising is that the writer stopped at Indians. Let's face it: world history is far more catastrophic than Treblinka or the Trail of Tears. Bangladesh, Tibet, Cambodia, Siberia...there's no shortage of suffering. If we began building monuments to commemorate all of the victims of programmed (or pogrommed) violence, we'd soon run out of stone.

Several years ago, the Israeli Supreme Court ruled that retired Cleveland autoworker John Demjanjuk is not "Ivan the Terrible," the horrific guard who tortured thousands in Treblinka. Witnesses and documentation haven't provided conclusive proof; Demjanjuk was either a reluctant guard or a monster, or somewhere in between. Who's to say? asks fellow Clevelander Martin Lax, who raised money for Demjanjuk's defense. "I might have done the same thing myself," Lax says—a mighty generous insight from someone who survived Auschwitz, whose parents were killed by folks not very unlike John Demjanjuk.

Does Demjanjuk deserve proper punishment for his sins? Certainly. But some people are crying not for punishment but for "justice." After fifty years and six million lives, justice isn't possible. Justice is fairness, making things right. And fate, with its usual sense of irony, has blended together the oppressed and the oppressors so we can't tell the compromises from the principles anymore. After fifty years, Demjanjuk is now "one of us" again. So is Lax. *But so is Ivan the Terrible,* whoever he was. The Victim and the Victimizer—history's yin and yang.

The Holocaust Memorial is more than a monument to one culture's brush with extinction. It is and should be a specific shrine to a unique crime. But it is also a metaphor of universal proportions for both Jews and Gentiles, uniting all of us in the memory of misery. For every victim of Nazi aggression—Jews, gypsies, Polish Catholics, the Russians in Leningrad—there were people who perpetrated it, people like my father who fought against it, and people who stood by and did nothing.

That would be us, your Honor.

The motto of the Holocaust survivors is simple: *Never again.* Native Americans—like Jews, like Armenians, like victims everywhere—deserve more than a monument. They deserve more than a search for blame, because finding the guilty is too, too easy. What they deserve—what we all deserve—is to confront the black night of hard questions, to peer into the darkness of our past and see ourselves among the aggressors and the aggrieved. If we continue to find solace in easy categories—we versus them, the Nazis versus the rest of us—then all of the memorials in the world will make one poor fortress when the hatred and the fighting break out. Again.

So Tender and Mild...

Christmas, 1994
with Beth Bateman Newborg

The interlude between Christmas and Lent is usually a quiet time for Christians. This year, though, as we lay away our crèche until next Christmas, as the liturgical calendar turns from the tender-eyed, nativity Mary to grief-filled Mary at the foot of the cross, we will be jarringly confronted with the TV image of another young mother who watched as her offspring died—her two sons, in fact. In the next few weeks, Susan Smith, the young South Carolina mother who strapped her sons in their car seats and drove them into a lake, will have her fate on earth decided by the courts.

Within minutes of her confession, the media and the public reacted with explosive outrage. Talk shows were immediately abuzz with condemnation. (Justice,

121

one caller said, would be best served is she were drowned in the same lake where her sons died.) A disbelieving disgust emerged: how could Susan Smith commit this unspeakable act...this aberration of human parenthood so unlike...well, so utterly unlike *us?*

There's no question that Susan Smith confessed to an act of outrageous horror, then managed to make it worse by manipulating the sympathies of both the town and the national media. No amount of rationalization can or should save her from her punishment.

Still, it troubles us how impulsively and completely we distanced ourselves from Susan Smith. Instantly, she became synonymous with the Outsider, with evil incarnate, a greedy, debased mutant. After all, *we* would never do such a thing.

That's true, we wouldn't. Most parents don't drive their children into freezing water in the middle of a weekday afternoon. But the comparison stops there. No survey would dare back us up, but our guess is that many parents—especially young parents with very young children—have *thought* about violence, have been driven more than once to the edge of the unimaginable. In fact, one would be hard-pressed to find a mother who, startled awake by the sound of her child crying for the umpteenth time on some God-forsaken night, *hasn't* had horrible, fleeting thoughts of physically stopping the relentless noise. (*I could take care of his crying for good...*) In the next millisecond, the thought fades, and the mother arises for the umpteenth time to soothe and comfort her adored, wearying, beautiful child. The child and the mother will make it through the moment without bruises; but should we deny that the crushing, awful thoughts were ever there?

How could parents who care for and love their children so completely be capable of such evil (if fleeting) intent? Perhaps that's the point. Such passionate, desperate love does not come without a price. Take a more common example: a child wanders off outside and is gone for hours. The frantic parents turn the neighborhood on its ear, searching for their kid. Yet at the same time there's a fierce anger. (*If I ever find Johnny, I'm going to give him a huge, long hug, and then so help me I'll...*) It's not a rational reaction, but logic doesn't enter into it. Intense love causes intense despair. It makes good parents crazy.

One could argue that the intensity of the reaction to Smith's confession bespeaks an increasing urgency to take swift social action against child abuse. But we wonder if, in our haste to denounce a mother such as Smith, we risk obscuring certain harsh realities of child rearing. One can imagine a young mother, at home on Christmas Eve morning with a couple of cranky kids, listening to this talk-show conversation (*How could she have done it, Larry?*) over and over again. When the news clips show the beautiful studio photograph of Susan Smith's dead sons, do they ever simultaneously run the phone number for the local parent/child guidance center? No. Instead, the young mother is haunted by the perfect image of Mary watching from the crèche. After awhile the present-day young mother would wonder about herself, feeling the awful, hot shame of knowing that, for one terrible split second, she understood something of what went through Susan Smith's mind. And soon it blossoms into the shame of confessing that she can't always handle her kids...while the rest of us, so judgmental in public, wrestle down the dark fear that hides within our private worlds.

For unto us a child is born.... Every year we celebrate the radiant, peaceful child and the young mother who found herself in desperate circumstances all those centuries ago. But we wonder (well, at least the two imperfect parents writing this wonder) how quickly any of us would have judged Mary's parenting abilities. Here, after all, is a mother who agreed to a rocky trip in advanced pregnancy. Had we been on the innkeeper's side of the door, would we have given up our room, our sure comfort, for this very young mother who had planned none too well or too far ahead? In cleaving the world of parenting into good mothers versus bad mothers, into rational parents versus the crazy, evil Susan Smith, we do little to nurture compassion for the less-than-perfect who come knocking at our innermost doors.

For unto us a son is given.... Do we have room to imagine what those words might truly mean when we are so determinedly making sure that the goodness of *us* shuts out the shocking imperfection of *them*? We see the peace and joy in the mild eyes of the sculptured Marys as we pack away our holiday manger scenes. Would we have seen the pain, the struggle, the guilt and doubt in the eyes of a laboring, flesh-and-blood young mother looking for peace and comfort on that night, or the thousand more frightening, worry-wrought nights that are part of any real story of parenting? Or would we have turned away from her, turned away from our own worse and better selves, sure that for the likes of *this* kind of young mother, our righteous hearts can have no room?

Elbows in
My Girlish Chest

There are two kinds of thieves. One type breaks into your home and indiscriminately steals anything of value, from the candlestick holders you hated to the napkin rings you loved. The other kind of thief is white-collar, the shyster in a nice suit, who chats and laughs and seems sincere as he sells you worthless land in Florida.

Depression is the smiling thief.

But unlike the real-estate swindlers who often prey on men, most dupes of depression are women. It's so widespread that it's almost considered a woman's disease, like toxic shock. But there's a strong (or should I say weak?) minority of men who suffer from the dual stigma of both "mentally unstable" (remember Tom Eagleton? Anybody?) and "not masculine." Men don't get depressed. Men get angry and frustrated and sometimes hit things—sometimes women and children—but they do not get depressed. They hike up their jock-straps, tell whatever's bothering them to kiss off, and move on. End of discussion. Depressions are only permitted after your team loses the World Series, you crack up your pickup, or your wife/girlfriend/mistress leaves you. You've got exactly 7.3 hours to get totally drunk while the jukebox plays George Jones, then it's back to work. If something is bothering you, you kick the son-of-a-bitch's *ass*. Depression? Depress *this,* pal!

Everyone who recognizes the smiling thief remembers where they were when they hit bottom. For me it was at the sink of my nice suburban home, populated by three children under the age of five and a lovely-but-growing-impatient wife, and all of it paid for by fifty-hour workweeks at three different jobs. (Guys work hard. Stressed? Stress *this,* pal!) The youngest child had colic, so I tried to fit my evening toilet between her bouts of crying. I had the toothpaste firmly on the toothbrush, but had suddenly lost the energy to bring the brush to my mouth. The nerves that caused my muscles to abduct and adduct had mutinied.

This is ridiculous, I thought, but I still could not urge my arm upward. I stopped trying for a moment, refocusing myself the way a basketball player does after missing the first half of a two-shot foul.

I tried again, but the blue fluoride just stared back at me, moored in the useless bristles.

Anyone else would've screamed by now, scared witless by this blitzkrieg onset of MS or ALS or some other terrifying acronym. But I know my enemy. He had snuck his way past my sleeping doorman and ransacked my hippocampus. The toothpaste now sliding off its post and into the sink was just a calling card after the burglary.

I should've seen it coming, but, like an alcoholic, you only realize when you've had "too many," never when you've had "just enough." For weeks, I had been either losing sleep or sleeping fourteen hours; I felt anxious about the strangest things—worrying about deadlines months away, meanwhile forgetting about a conference call just hours away. I had become slow and indecisive, letting freelance opportunities slip away through inaction. And, cruelest of all, my concentration suffered, making my already scattered synapses even more chaotic. I'd lose a train of thought in midsentence, or miss a crucial follow-up question during an interview. Instead of recognizing the symptoms, I simply grew more frustrated, chalked it up to the mayhem caused by my daughter's colic, and chastised myself to "get with it."

Despite these lapses and the concomitant moodiness, neither my friends nor my coworkers knew anything was wrong. The smiling thief keeps you friendly and entertaining. (The smile is sincere—I *like* to be with people who enjoy life. It's a vicarious balm.) But it still counts as stealing, despite the smiles: he steals your energy, your concentration, robbing you of precious weeks and months—all while you look and smell competent and collected. But once the smiling thief has made off with the inventory, there you are hunched over the sink, unable to brush your teeth.

In one way, I'm lucky. My form of depression, called "dysthymic disorder" (DD), allows me to be functional and nearly productive, versus the more severe, loony-toon depression that blows fuses and causes Blue Cross to raise its premiums. At least *I* go to work. I mean, it's not like I'm really *sick* or anything. (I've sometimes longed for the comfort and safety of hospitalization, instead of the half-alive feeling of DD.) It's like a low-grade fever or a simmering flu that makes your teeth ache. You're too healthy to stay at home but too preoccupied with dread to be at work. So you slouch from one appointment to the next, conserving your energy so you can smile and entertain as needed. As people get to know you, they detect that something's amiss. "Oh, you know," you reply, and shrug your shoulders with that unmanly thirtysomething angst. It's usually enough to keep them at bay—after all, no one really *wants* to know how you feel.

And that's the rub, isn't it? At least with a chemical imbalance, your moods are not your fault—surely you're not responsible for an overproduction of MAO. But DD denies you the luxury of victimization. No one can understand why you don't just snap out of it, and neither can you. Your superego holds emergency meetings to lecture you: "A loving family, a steady income, regular bowel habits, two cars with less than 150,000 miles—what more do you want? There are people worse off than you. You want to see *suffering?* Let me show you suffering…" And sure enough, against your will, you're watching the gaunt faces of Rwanda or pictures of AIDS patients or some other unspeakable horror. DD as Jewish mother. (A *real* man would say, "Guilt? Guilt *this,* pal!" But not you. You wimp. You fairy. In my dreams, George C. Scott is Patton, visiting me in the infirmary. "Your nerves?" he says. "Your *nerves?* Why you're nothing but a goddamn coward!" *Slap, slap, slap.* Wake up, you pansy, wake up.)

To be depressed isn't to feel disillusioned but enlightened. It's as if you've discovered just how hopeless and black the world really is. While the rest of your little universe celebrates birthdays and Stanley Cups and you, desperate to fit in, smile along with them, hoping some hope rubs off on you, you know the truth. There is no exit. Delusions 'R Us.

Thanks to advances in the diagnosis and treatment of mental illness, depression sufferers no longer have to worry about spending years in an insane asylum. Instead, they can worry about a new insanity called "managed care," an insurance practice that reduces both the cost and your chances of being cured.

My journey of a thousand miles through insurance red tape began with a single call to my family doctor. (I chose him because he had all of the credentials I look for in a physician: he was the only doctor approved by my HMO with an office nearby.) Now this doctor had an extensive background in psychiatry, having read Freud, M. Scott Peck, and *Sibyl*. When I told him about my symptoms, and told him how they mirrored signals from a previous bout with depression, he said, "Maybe you're just sad."

Yeah! That's it! And maybe that lump is just an abscess! And maybe those pesky chest pains are indigestion! And maybe you're a quack...

"No," I said, "I think it's more than that." Do *I* have to explain the difference between ennui and the black, optionless night of depression?

"Well, what should we do?" he asked, pretending I had some voice in this.

"Therapy worked the last time," I suggested.

"Let's start you off on some pills," he said, showing his high regard for my consult. "See if you don't feel better within a month."

Fine, I thought. And if I kill myself, I won't have to pay your bill.

Finding the right psychotropic drug is a lot like dating: some girls make you work, some do nothing for you, some make you comfortable—this one made me wish I weren't dating. I spent a month bobbing up and down like a hollow buoy at sea, tossed this way and that, mindless in my complacency. It's like bowling on Quaaludes—you keep throwing gutter balls, but you just don't care.

I broke through my medicated malaise long enough to call the doctor back.

"These aren't working," I said.

"Let's try another drug," he said. "Let's try…"

"*No*," I said. "Let's try therapy."

"OK," he said, very testy. "I'll set you up with a specialist."

Should have done that first, right? Not these days. These days, managed care makes doctors think with their pocketbooks first: drugs are *far* cheaper than therapy. Consider this: over the next several weeks, I had to run a gamut of "managed care interviews"—three different questionnaires administered by three different people on three different occasions. Sound inefficient? *Only if you survive all three interviews. Only if you don't say, "Forget it."* If a coupla patients decide it's not worth it and pull out of the process, the insurance company saves hundreds of dollars of pricey shrink time.

Worse, the interview questions themselves make you more depressed:

What kind of symptoms have you had?

Sleeplessness. Anxiety. Panic attacks. I know the script.

Have your symptoms affected your work?

In other words, any chance of us not getting our premiums?

How has your mood affected your marriage?

I am silent, unable to answer, trying to unhook the catch in my throat, trying not to think of how cruel I've been by simply not being there, by checking out so completely, even as I sit two feet away from her. Ten years of marriage, interrupted twice now by these black-hole sabbaticals, silences roaring like thunder through the bedroom. My wife becomes Saint Peter warming herself at the fire: "I do not know this man," she says, but no cock will crow to signal her blame. She is more the victim than me.

Have you thought of harming yourself?

This, the harshest question of all. Really they're asking, "Admit it, OK? Admit that you thought about how the edge of the barrel would feel against the roof of your mouth, the smell of the powder, the taste of the metal, the tension on the trigger, your last thoughts as you...*you wimp*. You coward. Go ahead, you fairy, pull the trigger. Just don't get any blood stains on your little pink training bra."

"Not really," I say. "Well, I mean not actively. Not altogether." I'm babbling now. Truth is, I don't know what I'm thinking.

But my answers must be right: yes, they think I should see a therapist. Twenty-five dollars a session, co-pay.

And the first thing the shrink suggests? More drugs.

But this time it works well, whatever "works" means. (Good antidepressants are like successful chemotherapy: sure you're glad they worked, but all in all you'd rather be in Philadelphia.) Prozac makes me better. I am neither whole nor well, but I am better. My wife and I can talk now. I sleep regular hours. I can concentrate. It's still like bowling on Quaaludes, but I can pick up my spares and add up the score all by myself.

And I'm making progress with the shrink. Out of the morass of conflicting impulses that guide my weekly sessions, I have fashioned this one prime directive: No more depressions. Never again. I cannot bear this again. Maybe two in ten years isn't bad, but they have aged me. I can't afford many more. I need to be stronger.

"Of course, *stronger,*" my shrink says, smiling. "Very macho."

I smile back, but for the first time I wish she were a guy. It's not "macho." Some things just are. Why do women wear makeup and panty hose? Cause it's up-hill if they don't. It's the way of the world. I didn't make the rules, and I'm not sorry about the Y chromo-some. I don't know why grown men still throw elbows underneath the boards of a three-on-three basketball game at the YMCA, but they do. Why ask why?

If my shrink were here (I sometimes hear her voice as I write this), she'd say this is more proof of my defeatist attitude: that I cannot envision changing my perspec-tive, but default instead to the ever-safe "That's the way things are."

We're both right. That *is* the way things are: for the rest of my life, it's a battle under the boards, me and the smiling thief.

For the moment I have the ball. I do not know for how long.

Grace in Free-Fall

My youngest daughter, Grace, is only fourteen months old, but already I have learned this: it is a miracle that our species survives. Other mammals begin to walk almost immediately—baby gazelles go from birth canal to twenty miles per hour in about forty-six minutes, otherwise they become some leopard's lunch. But human infants require enormous resources like food, Juicy Juice, and diapers for *months* before they even consider walking. And Grace's first steps are just as likely to be free-falls, slamming her little noggin on the corner of the coffee table.

So physically, at least, other species have one leg up on us. Sharks are such perfect eating machines that they haven't changed a whit in several thousand millennia; meanwhile, my daughter still can't figure which orifice gets the spinach—is it the ear, the nose, or the mouth? And mentally we're not much to brag about.

While salmon remember the site of their birth after three years on the road, we search every pocket upstairs and down, looking for our car keys. Bats use sonar to locate their two-square-inch home in a cave filled with a million other bats; we hunt through the garbage in search of a store receipt to Cousin Gert's too-small birthday present.

So why is it that we've thrived? We're no better physically, and some of our mental skills barely match those of a three-toed sloth. And God knows we're no more deserving. What, then, can we do that other species can't do better?

Laugh.

Cry.

Be ironic. Deductive. Introspective. Sinful. Forgiving. Contrary. Secretive. Circumspect. Inventive. Logical, outrageous, foolish. Kind. Violent. Simply: we can understand. We may err, we may even cause havoc—but the next generation can see our mistakes and right our wrongs. They can learn something beyond their instincts, beyond what they're programmed to learn. No other living thing has such capacity for wonder and synthesis and self-awareness. If it's not God-given, it is surely divine.

That divine self-awareness may well be the end of me. The same God who allows me to see the world's grandeur also turns my head to see the pain. I am often rocked by this imbalance, thrown off kilter. I teeter through this life, a tipsy correspondent in emotional free-fall.

I bring you news from the front:

I write this on September 8, a local anniversary. On September 8, 1994, a few miles from my house, USAir Flight 427 made its approach to the Greater Pittsburgh International Airport, then suddenly pitched left and went into free-fall, slamming nose-first into a barren hillside. There were no survivors. There were no whole corpses. There was nothing to do, save set up a temporary morgue and search for the cause, which, years later, remains a mystery. There were body bags. Ceremonies. A monument was dedicated. And still, still, still nothing to say. One hundred thirty-two people died on that plane—132 fathers, mothers, sons, and daughters, each with truncated versions of their brilliant lives.

Death is generic—even this sudden, mysterious, violent demise happens every day. Highways and alcohol chew up a couple hundred people per weekend, and who blinks? Are those lives any less divine? So why did I have trouble sleeping for a few nights after the crash, watching CNN far past midnight, far past the healthy point? And months later, why did I read the transcripts of the probe into the crash? What was I hoping for? An answer?

Present tense, September 8. I'm gripping the phone hard as a friend of mine describes the agony she feels about her struggling marriage. She even contemplated (briefly) an affair. But, she says, friends warned her away. "They told me that those kinds of relationships don't go anywhere," she says bitterly. "Tell me something: What relationships *do* 'go anywhere'? Where do they go? Do all relationships get better? Really? My sister and me didn't get along as kids, and we don't get along now. So what? What's that prove?" Her voice grows tired, resigned. "I mean, what do people *expect* of a relationship?"

I search for something to say—an answer?—but come up empty. Her life, my mind, and our relationship are in free-fall. We'll land, perhaps hard, on the ground, then go on. Because there's nothing else to do.

It's the last day of the season for our local pool. My two older kids, Faith and Hope, have learned to swim this year, and we go down to the pool for the last swim of the summer. After a few rounds of their favorite game, Try to Drown Daddy, they swim off to play with friends, and I sit on the edge of the water.

There must be 150 people crowded in this small space—all of them dressed in swimsuits, the closest to naked we ever get in public. The water in this pool, like life-giving water everywhere, dates back a few billion years to the birth of this planet. I watch the white skin and black skin and old skin and young skin troll and splash and dive and swim around me. There's a joy here, perhaps pressured by the setting sun, pressured by the knowledge of this, the last day before the coming chill. The shadows grow long at poolside. In these last few moments, with darkness approaching, no one here is seeking answers. Instead, everyone is swimming. The kids, young and old, keep playing, free-falling off the high dive, loose and boisterous in the buoyant water.

In the bathhouse, rinsing the chlorine from my faded swim trunks, I think: *It's not the answers that are important, but the questions.* It's not where we are that matters, or how we got here, or what to pack for the rest of the trip. Material things—a job, money—can offer us a car and gas and an open road, but sometimes life offers no reason for the journey, just an endless opportunity to wonder at the purity of it, the ineffable, crystalline madness of life itself. In an instant, it could end; would we realize what we had? Would we spend the final moments of our abrupt lives in slaying the dragons who told us to work more, to give up our time to anyone but ourselves, our loved ones? Because, left to themselves, relationships *do* "go nowhere." They must be cared for and dragged around and nursed and kicked and nurtured and jolted and survived.

It's all we have.

With every new word that Grace utters—*da, meow, clock*—she slowly joins the ranks of the conscious, the corps of the self-aware. It will be her greatest joy, her greatest penance. At birth she was little more than cutely wrinkled protoplasm; now she can laugh as well as cry, ask as well as answer, give as well as receive. The world is a fascinating place when you're fourteen

months old, and no one is more fascinating or mysterious than that funny kid who lives in the mirror, the
one who's so impatient, so inquisitive, so probing, so
human, so divine, so alive.

About the Author

Mark Collins is a part-time instructor of composition and literature at the University of Pittsburgh, an associate editor for *Pitt Magazine*, and a freelance writer and editor. His essays have appeared in *National Catholic Reporter*, *Pittsburgh Catholic*, *Christian Century*, *Pittsburgh Post-Gazette*, *Pittsburgh Press Sunday Magazine*, and other periodicals. He is the author of *On the Road to Emmaus* (Liguori Publications, 1994) and the co-editor (with Margaret Mary Kimmel) of *Mr. Rogers' Neighborhood: Children, Television, and Fred Rogers*. He plays left wing for the Relics and Chieftans dek-hockey teams and is tied for 989th on the all-time dek-hockey scoring list.